The CEO Strategy Handbook

G000241474

THE
CEO's
Strategy
HANDBOOK

STUART CROSS

GLOBAL
professional
publishing

Global Professional Publishing Ltd
Random Acres
Slip Mill Lane
Hawkhurst
Cranbrook
Kent TN18 5AD
Email: publishing@gppbooks.com

ISBN 978-1-906403-66-9

Printed in the United Kingdom by Berforts

Contents

Chapter 1

STRATEGY AND THE CEO

Remember, You're On The Bridge, Not In The Engine Room

Why You Need a Strategy

Congratulations!

I am delighted to tell you that your business has a clear strategy. Even if you don't think that you have one, or you think that 'strategy' is all academic nonsense, you will, nonetheless, have a strategy that is driving the decisions, actions and performance of your managers, teams and organization.

The strategy may not be obvious in your corporate documents, or even be clear in your own mind, but it definitely exists. If your sales' teams, for example, are consistently offering major price discounts, then you have a clear pricing strategy. Or alternatively, if, each year, you put off or reduce the levels of spend on marketing or technology, then you have a clear investment strategy.

The $64,000 question is this, however: is your strategy the one that you want, or is it one that has emerged, almost unnoticed, over time?

If it is the latter, if there is no top-down direction about how to deliver the future and ongoing success of your business, I can almost guarantee that your business is one that, over time, has had to learn to live with slimmer margins and frequent fights on price, and where any new activity is driven by the annual budget process – *What new things can we quickly do to add 3% to sales in the next 12 months?* – rather than as part of a coherent, ongoing approach to business growth.

Corporate success is hard earned for any business: there is no short cut. But if you are not clear about where your business should be headed, it is almost impossible for you to identify which opportunities to pursue and which to ignore, or how best to allocate critical financial and people resources. Done well, a clear and coherent strategy acts like a magnet being waved over iron filings, turning them from a non-descript pile into individual items that are all pointing in the same direction.

The good news, as this book will demonstrate, is that developing a business strategy need not been anywhere near as difficult, protracted or expensive as many consultants would have you believe. What's more, the process of leading the creation of a strategy that can step-change the success of your business can be one of the most enjoyable and rewarding things that any business leader does.

What Does A Strategy Look Like?

Here's my definition of a business strategy: *a framework for guiding decisions and actions across an organization to deliver superior performance*. Importantly a strategy is not a plan: a plan can fall out of a strategy, but a strategy can never fall out of a plan. A strategy is, instead a set of agreed goals, objectives and ways of competing that an organization's managers can use to shape and guide ongoing decisions, as well as helping them to develop specific programs and plans.

The fact that a strategy is a framework is why some executives don't believe they have a strategy when, in reality, they use it on a constant basis. A CEO of a rapidly growing $600 million retail business once said to me, *"I don't care for fancy strategy documents. We just do what we do."* He may not have been the owner of a 100-page, consultant-produced strategy report – lucky him! – but he certainly had a clear strategy for his business, which was, and still is, focused on three critical pillars:

- Offering customers the deepest product range;
- Delivering a lean, low-cost operating model with limited service and a focus on self-selection; and
- Pricing at a significant discount to their main competitors.

His strategic framework of deep range, low cost, low price enables managers and colleagues across the business to make decisions and take actions consistent with that direction. They know better than to introduce product ranges that demand significant personal service, or to propose opening stores where there are premium rents, but equally they are confident they will get support when finding new ways to reduce operating costs or adding to the range and choice for their customers.

My favourite strategy strap-line is that of Herb Kelleher, the founder and ex-CEO of Southwest Airlines. He described his company's strategy like this: *"We are the low-fare airline."* These six words helped his company transform the airline industry, as Kelleher and his team removed unnecessary luxuries such as seat allocation, free in-flight meals and business class sections. Each of these activities would have diluted the company's focus from becoming the low-fare airline and, over time, would have inhibited its ability to grow and prosper.

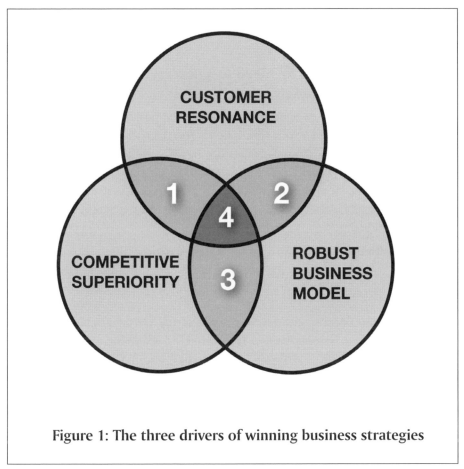

Figure 1: The three drivers of winning business strategies

As set out in Figure 1 there are three inter-connected factors that are necessary for a successful and winning business strategy which are:

■ **Customer Resonance.** *Are sufficient numbers of customers willing to pay the price for your product or service that allows you to make acceptable (or better!) returns?* At Southwest Airlnes Kelleher found a new, untapped market of independent travellers who preferred reliable service and low prices to the high cost of in-flight pampering.

■ **Competitive Superiority.** *Are you able to deliver your product or service in a way that is distinctively ahead of your competitors, enabling you to charge higher prices, drive higher volumes, or even both?* The gap that Southwest Airlines built up against its competitors has taken decades for others to catch up, and some of the US's traditional airlines have simply been forced to give up and fight their battles elsewhere. Other, newer rivals such as JetBlue may have closed the gap but have tended to have followed the 'rules' set down by Southwest.

■ **Robust Business Model.** *Are you able to turn your advantages into profitable growth by developing and operating an effective business model?* Unheard of in the airline industry, Southwest has delivered profits for nearly forty consecutive years. Some years have been better than others, but the focus of simplicity (the company only flies Boeing 737's to keep maintenance costs down, for example) and identifying low cost solutions (such as using cheaper local airports rather than more expensive international hubs) has enabled the business to create a viable financial model in good times and bad.

Unlike the Meatloaf song, merely achieving two out of three is bad, and from figure 1.1 there are various positions where you may find yourself. Which one reflects the position of your organization?

1. **Flattering To Deceive.** In Texas they have a saying, *"All hat and no cattle"* (I used to live in Newcastle upon Tyne in the UK, where the equivalent saying is *"All fur coats and nae knickers!"*). In this position you have a better offering than your competitors and customers respond positively to it, but you don't have the business model in place to enable you to deliver commercial success. In short, the more you sell, the more money you lose. Napster, for instance, was a ground-breaking business that first introduced digitally-downloaded music to the world. The bad news for Napster was that it hadn't created a business model that enabled it to work with the record industry and it was unable to turn its innovative, customer-pleasing proposition into a viable business.

2. **Lost In The Crowd.** Although you have an offer that customers like and have a sound business model, you do not have any real clear blue water against your competitors. The result of your 'me-too' offering is

that you will be likely to be forced to compete on price and will have to accept lower profit margins. For example, following Starbucks' success in added-value coffee, how many different coffee shop chains do we now see on every street corner? More importantly, how many of these offer anything different to Starbucks and are able to attract and retain their customers to allow the business to deliver superior returns? The answer is, of course, that very few are particularly viable.

3. **Table For One**. In this situation you have a truly distinctive offer and have a business model to back it up. The only problem is that too few customers find this offer sufficiently compelling for you to succeed! For example, I once helped to launch a new beauty store chain in the UK. Customers loved the concept and the experience they had in the store, but, unfortunately, too few of them came through the door!

4. **Lift Off!** Only in this position have all three factors come together to create a viable, growing and sustainable business. Zappos.com is one such business that has emerged in recent years. CEO, Tony Hsieh has created an on-line shoe retail business that has a clear and distinctive culture of front-line empowerment and a focus on 'wow' customer service. Critically, an efficient and effective supply chain that ensures timely and cost-effective order fulfilment supports Zappos' customer proposition. In less than 10 years the business grew sales to $1 billion and Mr Hsieh sold Zappos to Amazon for $1.2 billion in 2009.

Lead, Don't "Do" Strategy

Although CEO's see strategy development as a key part of their role, their detailed involvement can do more harm than good. There are three reasons why you should not try to develop your strategy single-handedly. First, you don't know everything. Allan Leighton, the former boss of UK grocer Asda (now part of the Wal-Mart empire) once said, *"I'm lucky if I'm right even half the time."* Seeking to have all the answers creates a dependent and, most likely, slow and unresponsive organization. Sharing the effort in developing strategy gives you access to a broader set of ideas and opportunities. You never know, you might even learn something!

Second, if you are seen as the sole driver of the strategy it inhibits others and prevents ownership. The problem with CEO-led strategy is that, to the rest of your team, it can feel like an order. You may get compliance – for a while – but will you get genuine enthusiasm, commitment and support? Involvement, on the other hand, helps you to build engagement and commitment, and improves your ability to establish clear accountabilities without everything coming back to you to make the final decision.

Third, CEO tenure periods are becoming less than the strategy cycle. According to Booz, the management consultants, average global CEO tenures fell from 8 years to 6 years between 2000 and 2009. This must mean that a significant number of CEOs leave their jobs within a few years. Consequently, there is significant pressure on you to deliver big results quickly, even if that goes against the best longer-term strategy for the business. Working with others can help you to remain focused on the real needs of your business, and avoid the possibility of being overly distracted by your own position.

So if you're not 'doing strategy' what should you, as CEO, be doing? In short, the answer is providing leadership. Here are 11 key roles for you to focus on in the strategy development process.

1. **Set the goals and ambition**. It is your job to say how high the bar should be raised. Managing the tension between what you believe is achievable and what your team feels they can 'sign-off' is a critical element of any strategy process. When he was CEO of drinks giant Diageo, John McGrath set his top-team a three-year profit target, demanded that the shape of profit growth be acceptable and insisted that the strategy should be in line with the company's vision. What he did not do was prescribe specific solutions – he wanted his team to create the answers and then deliver against them.

2. **Drive the pace of change**. Related to the overall goals of the business, the CEO must set the pace of change across the business. You will need to take account of the capacity and capability of the organization, but in my experience, if your people have clear goals and know what is expected of them they are able to achieve far more than even they believe. When Richard Baker became chief executive of the UK drugstore chain, Boots the Chemists, he sent a note out to his direct team. One of the points Richard made in that note was that it was the executive team's job to set the pace, avoid complexity and focus on success rather than perfection. The result was a step-change in the company's ability to get things done.

3. **Engage the top team**. We have already seen that the CEO can't do everything. Real up-front involvement of your leadership team enables them to take ownership of the future direction of the business and its

results. At an *fmcg* client of mine, the CEO used the top team to develop a refreshed strategy in a series of full-day sessions. The time spent by the executives allowed them to agree on the key strategic issues faced by the business and explore alternative routes forward. The result was an agenda with strong buy-in from the top team.

4. **Challenge and question your business unit leaders.** Engagement does not mean abdication. You can provide significant value to your team and your business by asking the critical questions and identifying the key issues that will drive the longer-term performance of your company. As you share your top-down goals, identify the questions you want each of your business units to answer during the strategy process. Then, as the team starts to develop their strategy, challenge their thinking to ensure that they have looked at real alternatives, and not just the easier solutions.

5. **Lead the debate about more radical alternatives.** In the end it is inertia that kills most organizations: they simply become too large, too inflexible and too risk-averse to make the changes necessary to remain relevant to customers. In my experience, most strategy reviews at the business unit level lead to growth agendas that are simply extensions of the current approach. The strategy can be summarized as 'more of the same'. It is up to the CEO to provide the impetus for considering sharper turns in the organization's direction.

6. **Lead the dialogue with the board.** Your non-executive directors and chairman will have a real stake in the company's strategy, and can play a positive role in offering guidance and providing specific skills and expertise. Keeping the board at arms length may seem more comfortable, but comfort and an effective strategy process do not generally go well together. Create a process that allows the board to review, challenge and provide input into the developing strategy. As with your team, direct involvement is the best way to create commitment. Having your board firmly behind you in more difficult times is much more likely if they have a strong belief in the company's underlying strategy.

7. **Ensure there is integration across the company.** In multi-divisional organizations, in particular, divisional leaders will, quite rightly, develop strategies that best suit their particular circumstances. Problems

can surface down the line, however, if you haven't ensured there is alignment and integration in certain areas, including:

- *Customers.* Do any of your divisions share the same customers? If so, how do their plans and strategies fit together so that the customer sees a seamless and integrated offer and experience?
- *People.* What people policies are your divisions pursuing and are these integrated? Who gets the first call on key talent to drive your most important initiatives?
- *Operations.* Can your back office operations support the activities of your various divisions? Are the divisions creating unnecessary stress in the organization by pursuing different cost/service strategies where one division wants to cut costs significantly and others want to maintain service levels?
- *Marketing.* If your divisions all fit within the same umbrella brand, do their strategies and customer propositions deliver the same brand values effectively?

8. **Align the strategy with the company's values.** Your people will understand and believe in your strategy if they can see a fit with company's underlying values. Zappos' success was a direct combination of strategy and values. The company's service promise simply could not have been delivered if front-line staff didn't share the same core beliefs and values about service. Everyone in the business had to be ready, willing and happy to find the best solution for customers without referring to a common script or asking their line manager to make the call. Zappos' recruitment policies reflected their values so that they could deliver the strategy effectively.

9. **Be the new strategy's role model.** Everyone across the organization and beyond will be looking at what you say and – more importantly – what you do before they will be persuaded that you mean business. It's not about having memorable catch phrases; it's about taking ongoing actions that are consistent and congruent with your stated objectives. Famously, when Boeing developed a strategy that was focused on higher quality, people only paid lip service to it until the key executive halted the production line so that errors could be corrected immediately rather than, as had happened previously, allowing the plane to move to the next stage and deal with the problem later. This

decision, which held up production for nearly a week, showed everyone that the executive was serious, very serious, even *uncompromisingly serious* about the strategy.

10. **Engage the wider organization.** I do not believe that the strategy development should be a democratic process; excessive involvement in the decision-making tends to lead to dilution in the clarity of the future direction. That said, the CEO plays a critical role in organizational engagement in two ways. First, you should be spending time on the front line with your workers and customers, understanding what is important to them and garnering their ideas and thoughts. You can feed these ideas into your initial questions and challenges. Second, you must take the lead in communicating the strategy. We will discuss this further in Chapter 6, but the key message is that strategy communication is not just about big set-piece events, but, far more importantly, is delivered through your daily interactions with people from across the business.

11. **Have the final say on big decisions.** It is your job to sign-off on the strategies, before seeking final ratification by the board; you must also have the final say on big investment decisions. Ultimately, the success of the strategy, or otherwise, will be down to you, so make sure that you have your say on the big calls.

As CEO of your business, are you spending too much time trying to have all the answers for your detailed strategy development and not enough time on being a leader? By taking a step back, allowing your team to take the lead, and then holding them accountable for results, you may find that you get both a better solution and more commitment to effective implementation.

Leading Strategy In Turbulent Times

In the post-war period up to the mid-1970s, the world, for most companies and business leaders, was fairly predictable. Steady economic growth led to rising consumer demand in most western markets, which, in turn, provided most companies with the opportunity to develop and market products that provided a reasonable return. During this period, 'strategic planning' began to be seen as a useful management discipline for many larger corporations, with the emphasis on 'planning'. Planning teams in companies such as General Electric, General Motors and Texas Instruments, began to develop multi-year sales, cost, activity and investment plans. Central to their ability to plan ahead in this way was their competence to predict, forecast and control future events. Forecasting economic growth, market developments and customer attitudes became central to the development of strategies and business plans.

Since the 1973 oil crisis, however, the risks of forecasting were brought home to planners and business leaders. Subsequent stock market crashes and economic downturns made the plans these companies had so carefully developed worthless. The level of turbulence, uncertainty and ambiguity that companies face has continued to rise exponentially, dramatically increasing the difficulty for CEOs and their executive teams to set out clear strategies for growth. Figure 1.2 sets out 10 drivers of turbulence that reduce any organization's ability to predict and forecast the future of their markets, limiting management's ability to invest with confidence.

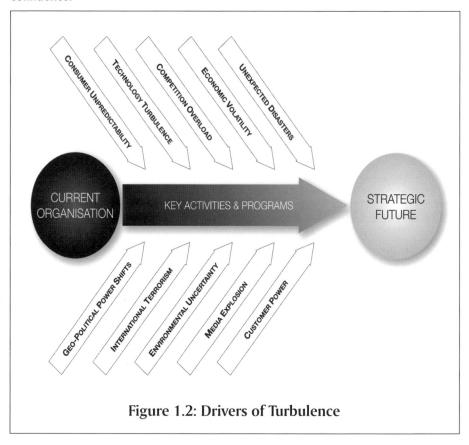

Figure 1.2: Drivers of Turbulence

The 10 Drivers Of Turbulence

1. *Competition Overload.* The level of competition in most markets continues to rise dramatically. Greater access to capital, new low-cost technologies and the increasing ease of international trade has created a relentless torrent of new product launches in most markets that make it hugely difficult to get your offer to be heard, let alone stand out. We are all just part of the noise. The growth of international competition, in particular, has changed the rules of the game. Even if you choose not to take your products and services beyond your national boundaries, your global competitors will be coming to you.

2. *Economic Volatility.* During his time as the UK's Chancellor of the Exchequer between 1997 and 2007, Gordon Brown boasted that his economic policies had ended boom and bust. Unfortunately, in 2008, his King Canute-style economic statements were ripped apart by the tsunami of the economic crash. In fact, since 1973, there have been a series of booms and busts, and unpredictable cycles of growth and decline. Finance ministers across the world appear to be relatively powerless to prevent them from happening and can only, at best, seek to minimise their impact on the more vulnerable areas of their economies.

3. *Consumer Unpredictability.* In line with economic unpredictability, shifts in consumer tastes and preferences can also be highly erratic. Following the 2008 economic downturn, for example, consumers kept their taste for high-technology products, but lost interest in environmental issues and ethically sourced products. They were still be willing to pay many dollars more for a leading edge smart-phone, but were less likely to pay a few cents extra for organic food. Knowing how consumers will respond to changes in economic wealth and product innovation across different product and service categories is definitely more of an art than a science.

4. *Technological Turbulence.* The pace of technological developments and the obsolescence of relatively recent innovations create conditions where it is increasingly difficult to determine the technologies in which you should be investing. Web-based developments have transformed customers' ability to review your prices and performance against your

competitors and, if necessary, work with suppliers and partners who are based on the other side of the world. For many CEOs, brought up in the era of slide-rulers, these developments can, at times, be barely comprehensible and somewhat frightening, but the pace of change continues to accelerate and new developments such as 'cloud computing', where companies use the web to access the IT capacity and capability of other businesses to deliver some of their own IT needs, will continue to revolutionize the business landscape.

5. *Media Explosion.* The web has also helped drive an explosion in the importance and presence of the media. Together with an eruption in the number of cable TV and radio channels, there is an unprecedented level of media space that needs to be filled with stories and opinion. From individual bloggers and tweeters, to the world's largest media behemoths, there is no longer any hiding place for your business. If you have acted unethically, even in an individual instance, and often when you have not, someone, somewhere will make sure that it is brought to life. You have no option, anymore, than to be totally transparent and authentic in your operations and communications. With this in mind it is perhaps unsurprising that one of the world's most valuable brands is Google, a company that gives people access – for free – to information from across the web.

6. *Customer Power.* The relentless rise in competition, the torrent of technological innovation and the explosion in media activity has served to put customers in the driving seat of most business relationships. Customers now have more information and more choice and the speed with which customer perceptions and preferences change can be devastating. For example, the level of trust in Toyota's products collapsed in a few weeks following the release of stories of problems with its autos. The company's faltering PR communications only served to make matters worse, and the company went from 'lean hero' to 'customer zero' almost overnight.

7. *Unexpected Disasters.* The forces of technology, media intrusion and customer power are brought together most tellingly when a company suffers an unexpected disaster. In 2010, for example, the terrible explosion at BP's Deepwater Horizon oil rig in the Gulf of Mexico and the subsequent massive leak of oil into the sea and surrounding

coastline created an environmental disaster for the region and a corporate disaster for BP. As websites streamed live, 24/7 coverage of the release of up to 60,000 barrels of oil a day from the broken pipes into the ocean, Tony Hayward, then BP's CEO, and his team acted indecisively and communicated poorly. The result for BP was that the company lost over half of its total value in little more than a month, faced a clean-up bill of at least $40 billion, and had to halt dividend payments and introduce the mass sale of many of its businesses and investments in order to fund the losses. But how confident are you that (a) an equivalent disaster couldn't happen at your business, and (b) you would be able to respond well in the face of such a situation? I doubt whether many CEOs or organizations would measure up.

8. *International Terrorism.* Since 9/11 the world has had to become used to cross-border terrorism. Most analysts believe that al-Qaeda and its affiliates will be active for a generation, at least, and their activities can have major impacts on how you will do business in the future. For example, which countries and markets do you wish to avoid because of their association with terrorist activity, what costs are you expecting to pay for 'safe' transport of your air freight, and how are you protecting your data and your customers' data from potential hackers?

9. *Environmental Uncertainty.* Despite the scientific efforts and evidence there is still uncertainty felt by a significant and vociferous minority of people as to whether the world's climate is fundamentally changing and, if it is, whether the change is primarily driven by the actions of mankind. As a result, governmental commitment to potential solutions has, in many countries, been sporadic, particularly in the US and China (the two largest carbon producers) and international agreements have been elusive. In such an ambiguous yet potentially critical situation, it is difficult for business leaders and their customers to know where and how to best invest for long-term success.

10. *Geo-Political Power Shifts.* Over the past 30-40 years, the US-Soviet Union duopoly has been destroyed and the US is left as the world's only true superpower. Its position as the pre-eminent leader of the free world is, however, far from stable. Since the 1970s, its power has been weakened by the relative rise of Japan and the oil-rich Arab states, and since 2000 economic and political power has shifted further eastwards, primarily

to China, but also to India and other Asian states, as well as Brazil and a resurgent Russia. The transfer of power is not done in steady steps, however, and the situation is highly fluid and unpredictable. The rise of these countries creates new market opportunities for many corporations but deciding where, when and how best to invest in these markets is a much tougher call.

'No Regrets' Moves In The Face Of Market Turbulence

In the face of this level of turbulence and uncertainty you may be forgiven for wanting to batten down the hatches and simply ride out the inevitable storms. Unfortunately, this is unlikely to be a recipe for success. On a more optimistic front, all the evidence shows that the companies who are able to consistently invest in the business, regardless of the external economic conditions, are those most likely to prosper in the medium and long term.

The key to successful strategy leadership in turbulent times is to be proactive and take control. The world may be full of dangers and risks, but it is also a source of endless opportunity, and changes in customer needs, economic conditions and technological innovations can provide the opportunity to create new, valuable revenue streams for your business. In fact, most business successes occur when a company becomes the first in its market to exploit the windows of opportunity created by shifts in the business environment. These companies may not be the first to spot the opportunity, but if they can be the first to take advantage of it they are likely to reap the rewards.

So what does this all mean for you as the leader of your business and its overall strategy? There are seven 'no regrets' steps you should take to drive the medium-term performance and strategic position of your company.

1. Relentlessly reduce costs and complexity

In real terms prices and costs always only move one way – and it's not downwards. Even in periods of growth and high profitability, perhaps especially in these periods, it is essential that you keep your organization fit and lean. McKinsey, the consulting firm, studied the performance of 1,300 companies as they emerged from the recession of 2001. They found that a critical success factor of the companies that gained or maintained their leadership positions had been their ability to control operating costs going into the recession. Future economic downturns will happen. Whilst you can't control when they happen or how serious they will be, you can organize your business to better manage your performance through the downturn.

If you wait until a downturn hits before you get your cost base into shape, it is likely that you will hit the easy costs – training and development, marketing, and recruitment – rather than the costs that will help you improve your performance on a more sustainable basis. Lowering costs when you are in a position of strength allows you to plan your actions, be more systematic, treat your people well and minimize disruption to the business. In short, by cutting costs consistently you can avoid, or at least minimize, the deep pruning that takes place with less systematic management teams.

A key and often-unseen driver of your operating costs is the inherent complexity of your business organization. Complexity comes in many forms, including:

- A significant growth in the number of product or service lines offered by the business, many of which contribute relatively little to revenues and profits;
- Excessive management layers and many managers having only a handful of 'direct reports';
- Lengthy and involved decision-making processes where 'sign-off' doesn't always mean that an investment has been agreed;
- Inefficient operational processes where different functions and departments work independently from one another, duplicating activities and effort;
- Unclear accountabilities and limited incentives and 'elbow room' for managers to lower costs, drive new changes and improve performance;
- A large number of corporate objectives and programs, each of which has to fight to gain support and resources from operational teams; and
- Too many performance measures, most of which aren't used to drive decision-making.

I can't put it any better than Arie de Geus in his book *The Living Company*. De Geus notes that all rose gardeners need to prune their garden to drive future growth. By pruning hard the gardener has a chance of spectacular growth, but also the risk that the flower dies from a late frost or other disease. Tolerant pruning, on the other hand, won't give the gardener the biggest blooms but gives a much better chance of roses every year. As de Geus writes, *"tolerant pruning achieves two ends: (1) It makes it easier to cope with unexpected environmental changes; and (2) It leads to a continuous restructuring of the plant that allows the rose to be stronger in the long run."*

What opportunities do you have to reduce complexity, drive down operating costs and accelerate profit growth?

2.   Increase your organization's speed and responsiveness

Convenience, speed and responsiveness are becoming increasingly important in our fast-paced, technological world. Finding ways to drive improvements for your business is a 'no regrets' move that is likely to help you attract and retain your customers. These investments and innovations are second nature to convenience-driven companies such as Amazon and McDonalds. Amazon, for example, now allows its customers to pay a one-off annual fee for which they promise next-day delivery on all purchases, and nearly half of McDonalds' restaurants are now open for 24 hours for at least part of the week.

But it's not just these convenience players who are driving speed and responsiveness; companies with different competitive strategies are also raising their game. One of my manufacturing clients, driven by innovation, also provides a next-day delivery service for its trade customers.

Specific areas where you can drive improvements include:

- ■ Reducing elapsed times to produce your product or service.
- ■ Making it easier for your customers to contact and buy from you.
- ■ Improving the turnaround times of your customer orders.
- ■ Lowering the time it takes to develop and introduce new products.
- ■ Rapidly resolving customer problems and after-sale issues.

What are the major blocks to increasing your company's speed, and how could you explode these barriers to step-change your responsiveness?

3.   Develop closer, trusted relationships with your customers

Given the level of choice available to your customers, and the ease with which they can now switch supplier, you must have clear strategies to find your customers, satisfy and retain them, and increase their share of spend with you. As in our personal lives, stronger relationships make it more likely that your customers will spend their hard-earned cash with you and stick with you when something goes wrong. It is far more difficult for your competitors to copy your relationships than it is for them to copy your prices and your products. In his book *Trust-Based Selling* Charles Green identifies four factors that help create trust and stronger relationships with your customers:

- *Credibility.* You are seen as an organization that can deliver your customer proposition. You have many satisfied customers and you are seen to have relevant skills and capabilities.
- *Reliability.* You deliver what you promise and, should any problems arise, you will sort them out quickly and without fuss.
- *Intimacy.* You are willing to share your inner thoughts, and are transparent in your dealings.
- *Low levels of self-orientation.* When you are with a customer, it is all about them not you. Your customers genuinely believe, and with good reason, that you have their best interests at heart.

What opportunities do you have to share information and knowledge, and get closer to your customers?

4.   Drive transparency and accountability

The growth in customer power, the explosion in media coverage and the ever-growing levels of unpredictability in the business world demands that you are transparent. If you have an issue, you must recognise it, own it, sort it out and communicate your plans and your progress. If you don't, then the media and your customers will do it for you, and that will not be in your long-term, or even short-term interests.

What are your plans to respond to a commercial or customer crisis, and how will you handle communication with your customers?

5.   Invest in partnerships

The high levels of turbulence in most markets, more rapid product life cycles, and the surge in specific technological developments make partnerships a critical element of any growth strategy. As the U2 song goes, *Sometimes You Can't Make It On Your Own*, and it is often better to share the rewards – and the risks – of new revenue streams with partners than it is to risk missing out altogether on new opportunities. Over the past decade there has been a rapid increase in the level of partnerships and joint ventures that leading companies develop. It is no longer just the high-tech industries where partnerships are the normal way of pursuing business development; they are now common in more traditional sectors. Procter & Gamble, the consumer goods giant, has, since 2001, turned its back on its traditional in-house focus for new product development and, instead, pursued collaboration with external innovators. The company now has a target that over 50% of new product launches are developed on the back of ideas and technologies sourced from outside the company. The company believes that its "Connect + Develop" open innovation platform will deliver $3 billion sales of additional annual sales. Bruce Brown, the company's chief technology offer, has said that the open innovation partnerships have *"changed our culture from 'invented here' to 'partnering for value'."*

Where could you use external partnerships to accelerate growth?

5.   Look for 'the next big thing'

When Steve Jobs returned as CEO to Apple in the late 1990s a business school professor asked him what his strategy would be. Given Apple's poor performance and weak competitive position at that time, and the fact that companies such as Microsoft and Dell had won the 'PC wars', the professor expected Jobs to say that he would be cutting costs, finding new ventures and improving product development. But Jobs didn't say that. Instead, he said *"I'm waiting for the next big thing."* By that Jobs meant that the markets in which Apple operated were chaotic, unpredictable and driven by technological innovation and that just because the company was down at that time, it could improve its position and performance by taking advantage of a new opportunity that would definitely come along. For Apple, the 'next big thing' was iTunes, and its success led to the iPod, iPhone and other product successes that have catapulted the business back to the top of Silicon Valley's list of winners.

What and where are the major shifts and fractures in your markets, and what 'next big things' could they create?

6.   Continuous, systematic innovation.

Given the level of change you are facing, the risk of not innovating is greater than the risk of innovation. Yes, some new ideas will not come off and there is always the potential that you will cannibalise some of your own sales. But it is better that you cannibalise your sales than have your competitors do it for you! Figure 1.3 sets out four kinds of organization and four kinds of CEO. Most businesses, in fact most people, are a mix of these four categories. So, ask yourself, if you were to divide all of your time and focus, what share would you attach to each of the quadrants?

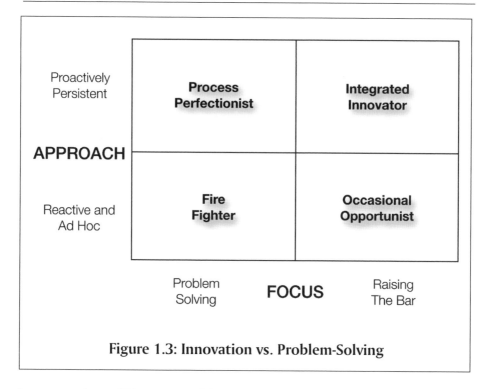

Figure 1.3: Innovation vs. Problem-Solving

In my experience, 70% or more of the attention of most chief executives is devoted to problem-solving, and up to 50% of it is on 'fire fighting', resolving issues as they arise. If you wish to drive a stream of profitable growth for your business you must devote a bigger share of your time and effort – and that of your organization – to systematic innovation efforts.

What All This Means For Strategy Management

It would be easy to decide that the level of uncertainty and unpredictability in today's world means that developing a growth strategy is a waste of time: you will be soon overtaken by events. Far better, you may conclude, to become as operationally excellent as you can, continue to cut costs and compete as hard as you can. The emphasis under this approach would be on consolidation, centralization, process re-engineering and lean management, often at the expense of brand and new product development or customer service improvements. But cost cutting and efficiency gains can only get you so far. Without ongoing top-line growth and a thriving, evolving brand, your business will quickly stagnate, performance will plateau and your organization will lose its ambition, its confidence and its momentum. The way forward is not to avoid strategy, but to change your attitude and approach to it.

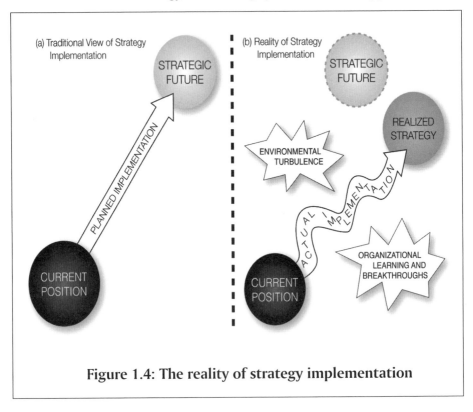

Figure 1.4: The reality of strategy implementation

Figure 1.4(a) shows a traditional view of strategy development and implementation. In this scenario, a management team identifies a future strategy for the business, compares that to the organization's current position and then sets out and conscientiously delivers a carefully designed implementation plan. We all know, however, that the world isn't like this. Perhaps there was some element of truth to this approach in the 1950s and 1960s when strategic planning first became popular in business, but even then I doubt it. It certainly isn't appropriate now.

Instead, as set out in Figure 1.4(b) delivery is usually a much more interesting journey! There will be successes and failures, and plans will need to change, often as soon as they've been agreed. The environmental turbulence we've discussed will constantly affect your organization and you will need to change course accordingly. But your final realized strategy is also driven by the learning and breakthroughs you encounter on the way. The end result is that you may end up somewhere near where you intended, but it is rarely exactly what you had in mind when you set off.

But here's the important thing. Without an idea of where you're trying to get to the turbulence and uncertainty you face along the way will mean that you would quickly become confused and lost. You end up like Alice in Wonderland, being told by the Cheshire Cat that if you don't know or care where you want to go, *then it really doesn't matter which way you go."* A clear strategy acts as a compass for your organization as you head through the inevitable storms. You may come across new opportunities along the way, find a better destination and change your route, but you should never be lost.

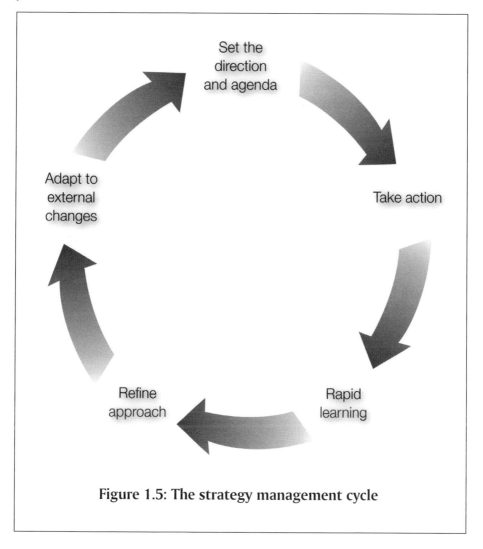

Figure 1.5: The strategy management cycle

As a result, strategy management should be an ongoing process in your business. You may have formal reviews and strategy assessments on a periodic basis, at least annually I would suggest, but you should review your progress towards your strategic goals and objectives, and your key initiatives, on a regular basis. These reviews should also include ongoing discussions and conversations about your ultimate destination. As set out in Figure 1.5, you will end up following a cycle of setting a direction, taking action, rapidly learning, refining your approach and taking account of external changes. The quicker and more regularly you are going through that cycle, the more likely you are to deliver strategic success. In that sense, strategy management is a Sisyphean task: like the ancient Greek king who was condemned to rolling the stone up the hill for eternity (only to see it roll back down again as he reached the summit), your job is to set goals, clarify objectives and drive action *ad infinitum*.

The rest of this book shows you how to make this happen.

Key Points

- Your business has a strategy, whether you've set one or not
- A strategy is not a plan but a framework for making ongoing decisions that help your company to sustainably improve performance
- Your role as CEO is not necessarily to have all the answers, but to engage your team to build a business that delivers profitable growth
- The level of turbulence in most markets makes the job of strategy development harder but no less important, and there are certain 'no regrets' strategic moves that most businesses can make
- In the face of this turbulence your job is to ensure that your business is flexible and agile, and that you are able to change your strategy in response to unfolding events

Chapter 2

STRATEGY'S SEVEN FATAL FLAWS

Why Strategy Gets A Bad Name And What To Do About It

Let me come clean. In my experience, many successful CEOs and senior executives resent the time they have to spend on developing strategy. There are two reasons for this. First, strategy is seen as being difficult. Consultants and academics have somehow succeeded in creating a misguided mystique around strategy that only people with an IQ of 150 or more and who have attended the world's best universities can do it. Despite the overwhelming evidence to the contrary that demonstrates that the best business strategies are created and led by pragmatic leaders who are willing and able to consider alternative futures for their business, many executives feel intimidated about their ability to create a credible strategy for growth.

Second, and more importantly, strategy development is perceived to be irrelevant to managers' daily and most pressing issues. Attending strategy meetings and retreats feels like a world away from the real work that must be done, and as the meeting progresses the frustrated executives begin to take a peek at their smart phones so that they are able to keep up to date on what's really happening with their business.

To a large extent, the frustrations of these executives are not their fault, but result directly from the way strategy is developed and managed in many organizations. I have identified seven 'fatal flaws'. By addressing each of these flaws, you will start to hardwire your strategy work into the real issues and opportunities facing your business. It will no longer be seen as separate to your ongoing operations, but will help your managers make better decisions on a daily basis, as well as helping you to make the big calls and create an organization that is able to thrive and grow.

So, let's look at each of these fatal flaws in turn.

Fatal Flaw #1: Allowing Planning To Kill Strategy

What is your reaction when you hear the phrase "strategic planning"? Are you energized by the chance to create exciting new opportunities for future profit growth? Or are you depressed by the thought of endless form filling, requests for further information, and periodic fights to protect your budgets? If you chose the latter option, you are not alone. I once read a consulting firm's survey that suggested that less than a quarter of senior executives agreed that they made major strategic decisions during the process.

Less than a quarter!

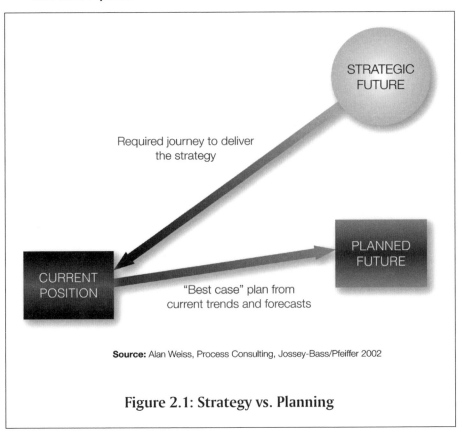

Source: Alan Weiss, Process Consulting, Jossey-Bass/Pfeiffer 2002

Figure 2.1: Strategy vs. Planning

In fact "strategic planning" is an oxymoron. It is virtually impossible to develop a winning strategy for growth during an annual planning process. Yet too many companies try, and fail, to combine the two tasks. The end result is typically a 1-3 year budget plan, not a coherent strategy for sustained and substantial growth.

Figure 2.1 compares a planning-led and strategy-led approach. Under a planning-led system, the senior management team tends to start the process with a level of growth that must be achieved in the next year or two to maintain momentum. Using a process that is generally led by the finance department it is, essentially, a budget exercise and the levels of growth pursued are commonly based on the company's current performance trends plus or minus a percent or two. Executives and managers may talk about the strategies required to deliver the results, but often they are simply dancing on the head of a pin. The big management discussions are not on major issues of strategy but on detailed budgetary issues, such as whether the gross margin target should be 32.4% or 32.5%.

In contrast, a strategy-led approach starts with a view of what kind of business you are trying to build. Your first tasks are to clarify how you can best win in the future, to agree your level of ambition for your company and to determine what size and shape of organization will enable you to make this happen. Once you have alignment on these issues, you can then determine some of the key steps you need to take to move you from your current position to your strategic future.

Using this approach you will end up taking actions you would never even consider under a planning-led approach. Paradoxically, it is often when companies are facing a real crisis that they find the resolve to use a strategy-led approach and break out of their planning-led incrementalism. At that point CEOs know that improving margins by a couple of percent will be insufficient to deliver sustainable success, and that bigger-thinking and more radical decisions are required. The problem is that by then it may be too late for the business to reverse its fortunes. Following the 2008 economic crash, for example, many of the US car makers that have been struggling to face up to international competition, finally made some of the major steps required to enable them to compete in the twenty-first century. However, having failed to arrest their decline over the past 20 years, there is no guarantee that these measures will be sufficient.

The time to drive strategy is when you're already succeeding and the best way to achieve that is to separate strategy development from annual resource planning, for four good reasons:

Planning vs. Strategy

1. **They answer different questions.** Strategy development is focused on how you wish to win in your chosen market, what distinctive advantages you need to make this happen and what capabilities and assets you require to underpin this approach. Although you will need a robust fact base to make progress, it is as much a creative process as it is analytical. Planning, on the other hand, seeks to identify the best way to achieve your objectives within the resource constraints you have. It is more about control than direction.

2. **They have different timelines.** Planning is required to ensure that managers across the organization know what resources they have, and what they are expected to deliver with them. A set timetable is required so that when the new financial year begins everyone understands what is expected of him or her. Strategy, however, responds to market issues and opportunities as they emerge. There is no annual timetable that can cater for these changes. It is not therefore surprising that few planning processes lead to major strategic decisions.

3. **They require different metrics.** The end result of planning typically comprises a profit and loss, capital expenditure and cash-flow budget, *possibly* supported by some market share projections. In short, the language of planning is financial. Metrics that help strategy development include, but are not limited by, financials. Innovation, speed, quality, customer satisfaction, loyalty, and brand strength can be equally valid measures. However, such metrics are often ignored during the annual planning process in favour of P&L projections.

4. **They involve different players.** Annual planning requires executive approval and sign-off, but can often be led by a central planning team working with line managers. Strategy development, however, requires the active involvement of the leaders of the business. Although support is required from other players, it is only when the leadership team has fully argued through the merits of different alternatives to future growth that clear strategic decisions can be taken. In short, strategy cannot be delegated.

Don't let planning kill strategy. By separating out strategy development from the annual planning process you will have radically increased your organization's chance of identifying new opportunities for substantial future growth.

Fatal Flaw #2: Incremental Thinking

Although a planning-led approach will almost inevitably deliver incremental gains, a shift to a strategy-led approach does not guarantee that major breakthroughs will follow. Incremental thinking is driven as much by your own mindset as it is by a particular process you follow. Taking a step back to look at your business is simply not enough; you must completely change your perspective and find ways to kick-start your brain into new ideas.

There are three key factors that drive incremental thinking.

1. An unwillingness to be wrong

An unwillingness to be wrong, or, more importantly, an unwillingness to be *seen* to be wrong, prevents many senior executives from proposing more radical alternatives to their existing strategy and business model. A *Business Week* survey once found that the most important factor driving the success of many of Silicon Valley's most successful entrepreneurs was an ability to 'experiment fearlessly'.

If you need to be right, and you aren't ready and willing to be wrong, you will only take incremental steps. You will never reach out far enough to take the actions that lead to step-change improvements. I'm not suggesting that you should take reckless actions, but without prudent risk there is unlikely to be material gain.

2. Unclear or limited goals.

Many of the organizations I visit either have no medium-term goals or have set a goal or vision that is so woolly that managers cannot possibly work out what needs to happen to achieve them. Instead, current year profit targets drive these corporations.

Now, I've nothing against profit targets. On the contrary, they help create focus and ensure accountability. However, if that's all there is managers will find ways to manage, and perhaps even manipulate, their activities to deliver the results required. A longer-term goal, and potentially one that is not purely focused on profits, can drive new thinking, different behaviors and greater commitment to the company's ongoing success.

The critical factor is that the goals you set are not driven by hubris or your ego, but by an understanding of what is possible for your business if you and your teams make the strategic and organizational changes necessary to deliver it. I once came across an organization that had set a goal of double-digit sales growth for each of the next five years. The only problem with the goal was that no one believed it, not even along the executive corridor. As a result, the final budgets that were agreed with the commercial teams were only half of the company's supposed ambition. Unsurprisingly, the rest of the business did not take the CEO and the top team seriously and within a matter of months several executives had left the organization.

In comparison, when Wal-Mart set a goal in the early 1990s of becoming a $125 billion business by the year 2000 (equivalent to three times their existing sales revenues) the executive team did so with a sincere belief that the goal could be achieved if they relentlessly and persistently improved and extended their existing business model. Success was far from certain, but it was at least possible, and the goal was rooted in a deep understanding of the company's capabilities and the potential prize that was available to the business.

3.   Resistance to changing the rules of the game

In the 15 seasons between August 1994 and May 2009, Manchester United, the UK's leading football team, played 286 home games in the Premier League. Of those matches, United won 212 and lost only 23. Visiting sides had, on average, an 8% chance of coming away from Old Trafford with three points, and a 75% probability of leaving with nothing but a poorer goal difference. Not only did the visiting teams have United's great players to deal with, but also crowds of up to 70,000 people or more, and match officials who may (or may not) have been intimidated by those fans, let alone United's manager, Sir Alex Ferguson, and his infamous stopwatch!

Few managers, planning their seasonal campaigns, look forward to the visit to United with any kind of optimism. And yet, many businesses operate in markets that are the equivalent of playing away at Old Trafford every week. Trying to imitate the market leader, they effectively end up playing to another company's rules, on another company's pitch, with another company's ball. Unlike sport, you are not tied to a particular set of rules, only to those that you decide to follow. Yet, in my experience an executive team is ten times more likely to invest time and effort in benchmarking the performance and strategies of their company's competitors, than they are in developing and articulating radical changes to create an organization that is uniquely advantaged.

Fatal Flaw #3: Putting Financials Ahead Of Ideas

Developing a business strategy relies on creativity and idea generation far more than it is driven by analysis. The reality is that most successful businesses start with an idea. Some times the idea is created in a *eureka* moment. Paul Allen and Bill Gates, who had been – mostly unsuccessfully – developing software for minicomputers, saw the cover of the latest edition of an electronics periodical, which showed a new, smaller computer that could fit on a desktop. They immediately realized that the future of computing was the PC and that they should focus their software development on these smaller, desktop machines. They called the makers of the PC and, within a few weeks, had written software for the machine and started a new company, Microsoft.

Other times the idea emerges more gradually. Fred Smith, for example, combined his post-graduate business studies, his general observation that most activities were becoming more automated and his experience as a charter pilot to develop the idea of an overnight parcel delivery service using a hub and spoke distribution model. Smith then joined the marines and it was only after he left the armed services that he pursued his idea with earnest, and created FedEx.

In both these stories, as in most business development successes, the idea emerges from individuals or small groups who have a strong desire to change the world in some way, and who are able to combine their expertise and experience in a particular niche with an insightful understanding of the broader changes driving the markets in which they operate.

Unfortunately, most of the books on business strategy have focused on analytical methods and tools, rather than how to create new business ideas or how to recognize and exploit your organization's unique experience and expertise. Contemporary models of business strategy begin with economic analyses, and strategy's leading authority is Michael Porter who, in the 1980s, produced two highly influential books, *Competitive Strategy* and *Competitive Advantage*, both of which are focused on analytical rather than creative processes to drive strategy development.

A certain level of analysis is essential for business strategies to succeed. But without a greater focus on ideas, you will simply end up with a greater understanding of your current market position, rather than a compelling basis for driving new profitable growth for your business. Figure 2.2 compares analytical approaches with creative approaches to strategy. Which best describes your strategy development processes?

Analytical Approaches	Creative Approaches
Focus on analysis of markets and performance	Focus on new ideas
Desktop assessments	Real-life experience
Follower	Leader
Problem solving	Innovation
What's happening?	What if?
Dealing with the past	Focused on the future
Financial proof before action	Action before financial proof
Forecasts and long-term plans	Rapid learning action plans
Strategy teams staffed with analytical experts	Ad hoc strategy teams staffed with a mix of 'thinkers' and 'doers'

Figure 2.2: Analytical vs. Creative Approaches To Strategy

One of the critical differences between the two approaches is that an analytical approach drives a need to obtain financial 'proof' before taking action. In the past I have sat in endless meetings where a manager comes to an internal forum to ask for some initial funds for an idea, only to be faced by a group of people with no real understanding of the idea being discussed, who then attempt to dissect it, criticize it and find as many reasons as possible not to do it. One of the initial questions this group will ask is *"Can you show me your business plan and financial forecasts?"* The meeting will then quickly descend into a detailed examination of the financials, rather than the quality of the idea itself. And if the initial financials are not deemed strong enough, even if the idea has real merit and could, if properly pursued, create significant growth, it will be dropped, often forever.

A few years ago I was working with a retailer that was looking for new growth ideas. One of the ideas suggested was to target a new group of customers through a non-retail channel. The potential prize was huge – up to 50% top-line growth. There was one problem, however: the initial financial modeling suggested that the profit margins would be only half of the margins delivered by the existing retail business. For that reason – and that reason alone – the idea had been dropped. It took a proactive and persistent commercial manager nearly a full year of negotiation with the executive directors to show that, if certain changes to the new idea's business model were made, the profitability could increase.

Even so, the new idea is being pursued with a fraction of the resource that I believe it warrants. If managers had put as much effort into learning about the new opportunity through rapid trials and low-cost prototypes than it did into writing more financial spreadsheets, both the company, and its customers, would be a lot better off.

How would these internal forums have dealt with the initial ideas of Sergey Brin and Larry Page, the founders of Google? The answer, we can safely assume, is not very well. Brin and Page would have been given short shrift by these risk-averse groups as it took them a couple of years or so before they determined how they could turn their search engine technology into a money-making business. For Brin and Page, as for most innovators, the idea is developed first and the business model second.

Until your business escapes the trap of seeking financial proof before taking action, you will always face a dearth of radical growth options and compelling innovations to drive your strategy forward.

Fatal Flaw #4: All vision and no direction

A vision is not a strategy. Unfortunately, many executives believe that creating a vision can equate to setting out a growth strategy. It doesn't. Your people may be inspired by your vision, but it won't necessarily help them decide how they should focus their efforts. Only when you have sufficient clarity that helps determine your managers' daily actions can you be confident that you have a strategy that is capable of becoming embedded across your business.

I once worked with a retail service business that had spent a significant amount of time and effort to set out a clear vision for the company's future. This vision was deeply held by the executive team and they had communicated it across the business. The vision statement went something like this: *we will be the best at what we do in the world*. The trouble, however, with such statements – that the company will be the best, the most admired or the avatar in its industry – is that they provide no guidance as to what you really want to achieve. As a result, my client's retail teams were carrying on as they had always done, and even the executive had not particularly changed its strategic agenda. The CEO and his team had not taken the next critical step of defining *how* the company was to become the best in the world.

Term	Definition	Example
Values	What's important to you about how you operate	**IBM**: Dedication to every client's success; Innovation that matters, for our company and for the world; Trust and personal responsibility in all relationships
Mission	Why your organization exists, over and above making money (also called your core purpose)	**IKEA**: To create a better everyday life for the many people.
Vision	An inspirational, over-arching long-term future goal	**SAMSUNG**: Inspire the world, create the future.
Strategy	A framework for guiding decisions and actions across your organisation to deliver superior performance and your vision	**BMW**: The BMW Group is the leading provider of premium products and premium services for individual mobility.
Plan	The allocation of resources to implement an agreed set of actions	**FIFA**: Russia will host the 2018 World Cup and must deliver the plan set out in the bid document

Figure 2.3: Strategy-related definitions

Figure 2.3 sets out definitions for several strategy-related terms that are often confused. Samsung's vision, for example, which states that the company will *"inspire the world, create the future"*, can help its executives and teams to raise the bar on their current levels of performance but it doesn't articulate the markets in which the company will participate or which customers it is targeting.

BMW's simple strategy statement gives a clearer sense of where and how the company should be operating. It gives guidance about how managers should be operating, but is not completely restrictive. For example, its market or business domain is 'individual mobility'. This means the automobiles and motorcycles the company already produces, but could potentially include pedal-power bicycles or even personal jets in the future. The inclusion of 'services' as well as 'products' certainly means it will deliver its current range of financial services, but again does not preclude the offering of broader transportation services. In short, the strategy statement provides a framework for what the current business is, but also how it might evolve in the coming years.

Fatal Flaw #5: A Failure To Make Trade-Offs

The corollary of identifying the core of your strategy is deciding what you're not, and what's of less importance to your business. At this point we reach the dreaded word in strategy development – *trade-off*. If you are unwilling to make clear and proactive trade-offs, it is unlikely that you will have a leading position in your market or a winning strategy.

So why is this so hard? The answer is simple. Making trade-offs means that you're giving something up and, if you're not 100% confident in your stated strategy, it is more than tempting to hedge your bets, have a look at what the competition is doing and say to yourself "*Let's try a bit of what they're doing*." The result is that your own business spends all its time keeping up with the Joneses, rather than trying to create something that is distinctive and uniquely valuable.

When I was growing up my older brothers and I used to finish our meals as quickly as possible in the hope of getting some of the food from my younger brother's plate. Once we had eaten our dinner we would intently watch him eat every mouthful, silently willing him to put down his cutlery and finish his meal. Whenever he left some food we would collectively pounce on his plate and fight for the scraps that remained.

There is an old medieval word for our behavior of silently and longingly staring at someone else's food in the hope of being offered it: it's called *groaking*. And it's not only greedy, adolescent schoolboys who *groak*. Many business executives look longingly at their competitors, wanting what they have. In particular, they look to copy the market leader in a bid to enjoy a bit of their meal.

Corporate *groaking* (you might call it competitive benchmarking) results in competitors becoming pale imitations of the #1 player. In the UK coffee shop market, chains including Café Nero, Costa, Eat, Coffee Republic, Coffee Primo, Café Ritazza and other local cafes were established in the hope of enjoying some of Starbucks' success.

The problem for the challengers is that in most markets it is only the leading players that make meaningful returns. It is the leaders that occupy the biggest share of buyers' attention and spend. Unless something dramatically different comes along that is clearly better than their current provider potential customers will be unlikely to notice 'me-too' suppliers.

By seeking to copy the leaders, these challengers end up fighting over scraps in much the same way as I did with my brothers. It is unsurprising that many of the players in the coffee shop market have either performed poorly or even ceased trading. There are two tests of your customer proposition and business model you should apply to understand whether you are equipped to grow profitably:

1. *Are you distinctive?* Do you offer something that is dramatically different to other players in the market? Is there something unique and compelling about your proposition or business model that customers immediately notice? For example, Dell offers fairly standard PC's and laptops, but provides customers with low prices, customized specifications and delivery direct to their home or the office.

2. *Are you advantaged?* Are you able to turn this distinctiveness into superior performance? Can you create a system to deliver your proposition that others will find difficult to copy? Over time Dell has built and refined a business model that is completely aligned with its source of distinctiveness and which has created and sustained its advantage over its competitors. For example, building-to-order has allowed Dell to align its suppliers into a 'just-in-time' supply and manufacturing system, significantly reducing the company's working capital, improving its cash flow and increasing its return on investment.

Fatal Flaw #6: Insufficient focus on action

Few, if any strategies emerge from implementation unscathed. By pursuing your big objectives, implementing your initial plans and taking action you are likely to change, in some way, the direction you have set. It is only by learning from your actions that you can really clarify how you can best succeed in the future. The results of your actions will drive your strategy at least as much as your strategy drives your actions. The ideal cycle of idea generation – action, learning and refinement – is set out in Figure 2.4. The critical aspect of this cycle is to learn as quickly and as cheaply as you can. Your ability to create competitive advantage is, to a large extent, driven by your ability to operate this cycle faster, cheaper and more effectively than your rivals.

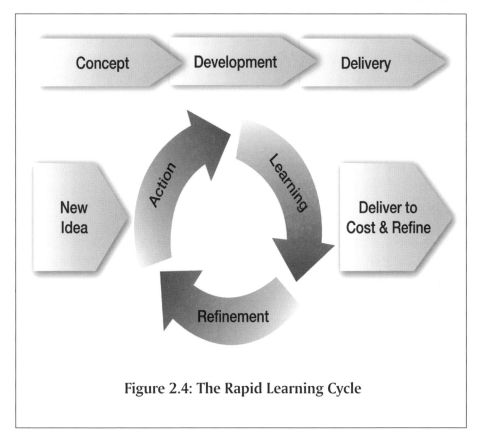

Figure 2.4: The Rapid Learning Cycle

However, the pursuit of planning ahead of strategy, a bias towards incremental thinking and the need for financial proof ahead of the desire to develop new ideas, all mitigate against taking action. Instead, managers spend their time perfecting their financial models and plans and only commence delivery once they are confident that success is virtually guaranteed. That usually means that, even in the initial trial phase, the focus of the project is on hitting a particular financial target rather than maximising learning. If there is any risk that the financial target won't be hit, then the trial will not be sanctioned and no action will take place.

The problem with this approach is that the managers are asking the wrong question. In the early stages of developing new business ideas you should not be asking, *"Can we make sufficient returns in this area?"* but should, instead, be asking these questions:

- *Is this idea likely to help us to become a market leader?* If the idea only helps you to play catch-up, and produces a me-too offer that imitates what's already out there, it may help you keep up with the pack but it's unlikely that it will transform your performance. If you have an idea, however, that could take your business to the forefront of your industry, you are likely to create the energy and focus for your organization that can't help but drive action.

- *Do sufficient numbers of customers like this idea?* If they don't, then by all means you should kill the idea (although you may find that by refining it you get a different customer reaction), but if your initial trials suggests that you have a potential winner on your hands, you can then begin to work out how to create an attractive business and financial model.

- *How do we make the idea technically feasible?* Prototyping your products, services and processes is a critical element of driving your strategy forward. Over a five-year period James Dyson made over 5,000 prototypes of his revolutionary bagless vacuum cleaner before creating a fully trademarked, production version.

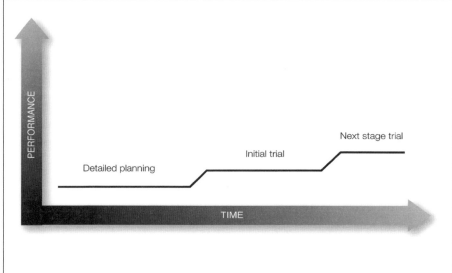

Figure 2.5a: How An Action-Based Approach To Strategy Succeeds – Traditional Approach

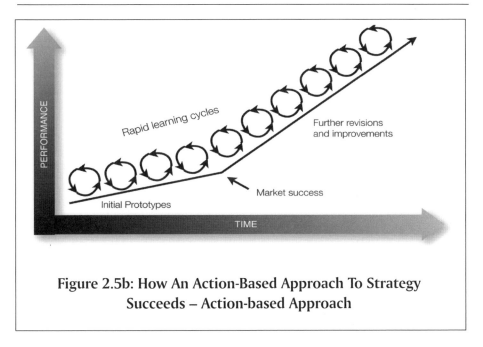

Figure 2.5b: How An Action-Based Approach To Strategy Succeeds – Action-based Approach

By changing the questions you ask you are more likely to drive action, learn how to succeed and actually achieve something. Figure 2.5 demonstrates the difference between the two approaches. At its heart is a shift in managerial mindset from one of risk aversion and a need to have as many questions answered before doing anything, to one where trial and error and learning through action drives a succession of prototypes and versions that drive your business forward. In his book, *Bloomberg By Bloomberg*, Michael Bloomberg, the founder of the eponymous financial information and media empire, put it like this, *"We made mistakes of course. Most of them were omissions we didn't think of when we initially wrote the software. We fixed them by doing it over and over, again and again. We do the same today. While our competitors are still sucking their thumbs trying to make the design perfect, we're already on prototype version No. 5. By the time our rivals are ready with wires and screws, we are on version No. 10. It gets back to planning versus acting. We act from day one; others plan how to plan – for months."*

Fatal Flaw #7: An overreliance on external consultants

The final fatal flaw that undermines business strategy is a reliance on external consultants. As a consultant myself I know that, done well, working with external consultants can add real value to the development and delivery of your business strategy. The problems arise, however, when CEOs and their executive teams start to rely on these consultants for strategy, rather than working with them as partners. This means that instead of asking the consultants for help with process and for input on ideas, managers end up delegating to the consultants the overall strategy itself.

Such reliance creates the following problems for executive teams:

- **Lower levels of management involvement and ownership.** Developing and executing a great business strategy can be time-consuming and hard work. But it is a key job of your managers, and, behind all the jargon, is less difficult to do than many managers believe. By all means get external support where this makes sense, but a commitment to action is driven by a sense of ownership of the strategy, and that sense of ownership is, in turn, driven by involvement. The most successful businesses I have worked with all have a huge sense of ownership of their strategy, and although their top team may work with external advisors, it is the leaders that take the lead in setting the direction, determining the big goals and taking accountability for their delivery.

- **A focus on analysis ahead of action.** Many consultants have followed a traditional business school education, which emphasises analytical tools and approaches. Unsurprisingly, these consultants tend to focus their efforts on analysing data and producing information packs, rather than helping the company's managers and teams to take action. I am sure that you have seen the data-rich 'decks' that consultants produce and which, more often than not, lie undisturbed in the CEO's filing system for years after the work is complete. It's not that the analysis is not accurate, but that it just doesn't help move the business forward.

- **A me-too strategy.** Consultants, under pressure to demonstrate their expertise, share their knowledge of their clients' key markets and identify what others have done to succeed as the basis of their recommendations for growth. Their insights and recommendations are fine as far as they go, but they will not create true distinctiveness. It is difficult to imagine an external consultant recommending breakthrough business ideas such as Apple's iTunes, Facebook or, in a previous decade, Renault's distinctive design of its family of automobiles. Each of these business decisions carried too much risk to be made by consultants, and relied on the trial-and-error, action-based approach that market leaders and innovators pursue, and that can only be driven by the company's executives and managers.

By all means work with trusted consultants to aid and accelerate your strategy process, and to offer ideas and challenges to your company's internal thinking and priorities. But do not let the consultants take over. If you ever believe that the consultant rather than your team has set the agenda for a strategy meeting, you should start to be concerned. Do not be afraid of strategy – the techniques and approaches in this book can help you take hold of the steering wheel and make sure that you are in the driving seat, not the back seat, when setting the future direction of your organization.

Key Points

There are seven fatal flaws that you must avoid if you are to create and deliver an effective, high-value strategy:

- Fatal Flaw #1: Allowing planning to kill strategy;
- Fatal Flaw #2: Incremental thinking;
- Fatal Flaw #3: Putting financials ahead of ideas;
- Fatal Flaw #4: All vision, no direction;
- Fatal Flaw #5: A failure to make trade-offs;
- Fatal Flaw #6: Insufficient focus on action; and
- Fatal Flaw #7: An overreliance on external consultants.

Chapter 3
CREATING A STRATEGY WITH CUT-THROUGH

From Empty Clichés To A Clear Direction

Don't Look At The Future From Where You Are Now

When I was a child I used to do puzzles that gave me five possible ways of getting from A to B, only one of which was possible. Over time – probably several years! – I realised that the easiest way to solve the puzzle was to start at B and work back. Tracing the line with my pencil would automatically take me to the right answer, and avoid unnecessary time testing out all the other options.

The same is true of business strategy. Perhaps counter-intuitively, the starting point of strategy should be your end point. Without having an understanding or view of where you want to be, you will have no idea whether you are on the right path. Unfortunately, many executive teams spend inordinate time and expense on assessing their current performance, and finding ways to improve it by a few percentage points, without having a clear view of what level of performance they really need to succeed. They have too many plans and too little strategy. If, instead, they spent a bit of focused time and effort defining their ambition for the next few years, they would be in a much better position to assess whether they needed to improve what they were already doing, or focus on doing something completely different.

These teams behave like a couple on a driving holiday who, despite touring without any specific destination, are constantly tracking where they are on the map, what speed they are going, and how many miles per gallon they are getting from their tank. These factors may be interesting and they may find ways to improve their speed and fuel efficiency, but these measures become infinitely more useful when you decide where you want to go. Once you have clarified your destination you can quickly work out if you are on the right route, how long it will take to get there and how much it will cost.

Unlike a 'normal' planning exercise, which takes your current position and performance and extrapolates them into the future, a strategy-led approach first sets a clear destination and then works backwards to find the quickest and safest route to get there. Once you have done that you can see if your current growth path is likely to get you anywhere near where you want to go, or if you are going to have to drop some of the things you are doing and, instead, focus on a completely different set of activities.

For example, back in the 1980s, the new boss of GE, Jack Welch, famously told his divisional bosses that they needed to become number one or two in their markets or he would sell their companies. The clarity of Welch's objective forced his managers to radically reappraise their performance and strategy. Where they believed they wouldn't achieve the necessary market position they did something about it. They didn't simply work harder at what they were already doing; they fundamentally changed the way their businesses operated. New acquisitions and investments, growth initiatives, profitability improvements and business ideas were put on the table and delivered, and, as a result, GE's market value grew eleven fold between 1990 and 2000, from $50 billion to $560 billion.

Why Most Vision Statements Have No Cut-Through

We have already discussed the fact that many executives confuse 'strategy' and 'vision'. Personally, I'm not a huge fan of vision statements. In my experience the vision statements of many organizations have no resonance outside the board room. They may mean something to those executives who developed the statement (or delegated the development of it), but, in many cases, is too input-focused and generic to be of any real use to people at the front-line. The trouble with statements that state that the company will be the best, the most admired or the avatar in its industry is that they provide no guidance as to what you really want to achieve.

Take these randomly selected vision statements from four of the UK's leading retail banks. I am not picking on this industry. On the contrary, I think that these statements reflect the quality and style of many corporate visions across a variety of sectors. The four visions are:

1. To become one of the handful of universal banks leading the global financial services industry
2. To be the best financial services organization in the UK
3. To be the UK's most admired financial services business
4. We are the world's local bank

Only the fourth statement, which is HSBC's vision statement, gives me a sense of direction. When I read that vision, I get a sense of a global presence, an interconnected organization and a focus on strong customer relationships. I imagine that senior management comprises people from diverse backgrounds who are brought together by their cosmopolitan approach. With the other banks, too much is left out. In particular, I have no inkling as to *how* they are seeking to achieve their goal. The only picture it brings to my mind is of a lot of middle-aged men in pinstriped suits, crisp shirts and red braces. If their vision statement were an arrowhead it would simply bounce off its target rather than cut through it. Perhaps it's no surprise that HSBC performed best of these four through the 2008 banking crisis.

From The Top: Jeremy Ling

Jeremy Ling is the CEO of The Bristan Group Limited, the UK's largest bathroom taps/faucets and showers company, and a subsidiary of the $8 billion US-based Masco Corporation, one of the world's largest manufacturers of brand-name products for the home improvement and home construction markets.

I have held several senior leadership positions during my career and have always appreciated the importance of having a clear business strategy that is based on robust consumer and market insights. That said, since joining Bristan I have learned three major lessons:

1. **There is a huge advantage gained by involving more people in the strategy process.** *As you start a new strategy development process, one of the first questions you need to answer is "Who should I involve?" Historically,*

I have focused on working with the top team, but I have now learned that you can go a lot further than that. We developed our business strategy by directly involving over 40 senior managers in its creation. The CEO and other senior executives cannot capture the level of knowledge that facilitates really robust strategic plan development. I have learnt that middle managers are very willing and able to face into our company's biggest, most challenging issues – they came up with creative, value added solutions that challenged the thinking of our executive team. What's more, their involvement in the process has step-changed their level of engagement with the business and their commitment to the delivery of the strategy.

2. **Your strategy must be constantly evolving.** *We spent a great deal of time developing our business strategy, and its related plans and programs. Since its formal sign-off, however, we have found that we must constantly challenge and refresh it. The core of the strategy and its performance goals has remained pretty consistent, but we have revisited and changed some of the specific decisions we made at that time. These changes haven't happened in a formal strategy review process, but as part of the normal management processes of the business – management team meetings, business review and departmental meetings. The benefit of establishing a clear strategy is that it forms the basis of our meetings and so we are able to shape it through our ongoing conversations and dialogues, and not just through set-piece events.*

3. **Delivery of your company strategy takes place through individual actions.** *At the same time as we developed our company strategy we reviewed our organisational structure and established four market-facing divisions supported by*

our back-office and corporate teams. Each of these divisions has their own set of performance objectives and programs, but we have made sure that we have driven accountability further. Every one of our 700 employees has a performance contract that is shaped directly by their specific contribution to their division's strategic agenda. Their job descriptions, performance objectives and bonus criteria reflect their impact on the division's KPIs and their involvement in its strategic projects. That way, we ensure that we align our corporate goals with individual objectives, and the subsequent performance review conversations provide a feedback loop on the effectiveness of our strategy, allowing us to continue to improve it as we go along.

Creating A Strategy Arrow

Rather than creating meaningless vision statements I believe your time is far better spent building and clarifying your strategy for growth. An old boss of mine used to tell me, *"Stuart, if you can't describe the issue you'll never solve it."* It's the same with strategy. If you can't describe it to your organisation in plain, straightforward terms then they'll never be able to make it happen.

A statement of your strategy must be clear, specific and concise. It is not a high level vision, which describes what kind of organisation you aspire to be (e.g. *To be the world's greatest airline*) or mission, which sets out why your organisation exists in the first place (e.g. *To help people lead healthier lives*). It is, instead, a description of what your business will focus on to drive its success over the next few years. As set out in Figure 3.2 there are four elements to an effective strategy statement:

1. Your #1 Goal;
2. Where You Will Play;
3. How You Will Win; and
4. Your Agenda For Action.

Let's take each of these in turn, using the experience of one of my clients (we'll call the company *ServiceExcel*), that operates in the services market.

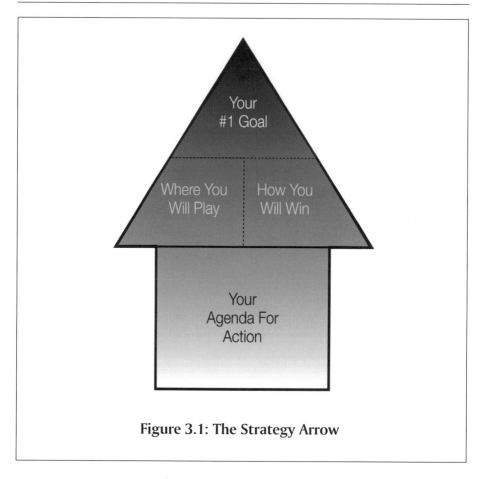

Figure 3.1: The Strategy Arrow

Your #1 Goal

As we've discussed a strategy is only relevant when it has a clear goal that it is seeking to deliver. Your first step is therefore to establish a clear goal for your business. You will have several important goals that you want the business to deliver, but which of these is the most important to your long-term success? This approach is the opposite of the widely used 'Balanced Scorecard'. My problem with the Balanced Scorecard approach to strategy and performance management is that it is, well, too balanced. It makes everything of equal importance. In most Balanced Scorecard projects and reports I've seen, there is a general assumption that all goals carry the same weight. The end result is that the management of the business becomes unnecessarily complex and confused, with managers trying to keep on top of a dozen or more measures.

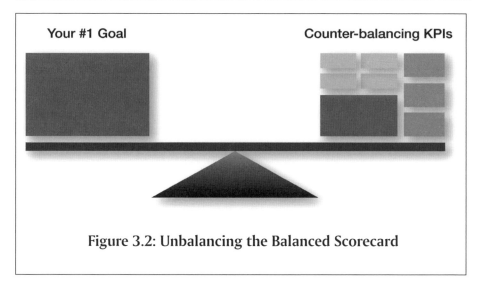

Figure 3.2: Unbalancing the Balanced Scorecard

When I work with my clients we determine what their #1 goal is, and use that goal to drive our agenda and strategy. We then identify other KPIs to counter-balance our goal and make sure that it is delivered in the right way, but we don't give everything equal weighting. As set out in the Figure 3.2, it is like having one major weight being counter-balanced with several smaller weights. In that sense, our scorecard is purposefully unbalanced. The advantages of this approach are that it gives you and your team a clear focus for improvement, aids communication across the organization, helps you make better and quicker strategic and resource allocation decisions and accelerates organizational momentum.

In fact, I would argue that identifying and embedding your #1 goal is the most important strategic decision you will make. Even if you do nothing else I recommend in this book, clarify your top goal and you will find that everything else will start to align around it.

There are three questions you need to answer to establish your #1 goal.

1. What is the best metric to use?

The first decision you need to make is what metric you will use to set the goal. The key to establishing a lasting goal is to ensure that the metric is based directly on the key drivers of your company's economic engine. What, if you focus on it fully, will best deliver the growth, profit and returns you're after? Most of the executive discussions I am involved with consider the following areas:

- **Profit**. A profit goal is relatively easily measured for most organizations and is, of course, the most common corporate success criteria. It is also the most widely used goal metric I have come across. Its advantages include the fact that, for most companies, it is already closely measured and monitored and that profits are the final outputs of all management decisions and is, in that sense, comprehensive. It is also relatively easy to link individual and team rewards to profit performance. The downside of using profits, however, is that it can be achieved (and manipulated) by a variety of levers, including accounting policies. So, you may find that in a difficult trading year you focus on delivering the profit number by cutting important investments, even though that may not be in the best longer-term interests of your business.

- **Sales**. A sales goal is even more easily measured than profit, and is also easier for your front-line teams to understand. For most companies, sales revenue is also the biggest driver of profits and value. That said, a sale at any price destroys rather than builds value, and it is easy to give away sales too cheaply if that is your key goal.

- **Size**. Some companies set other size-based goals as their #1 target. This may be in the form of market share or position (as with GE), market capitalization or even number of locations, and is based on the insight that there are scale economies and competitive advantages available to most businesses if they can reach a certain magnitude.

- **Customers**. Customer-focused goals are increasingly popular. These can be in the form of absolute customer numbers, share of your customers' spend or customer satisfaction, retention and loyalty. These goals are based on the insight that increasing customer loyalty drives profitable growth and that, after all, the ultimate purpose of your business is to identify and serve your customers. As with sales goals, however, it is important that the goal is not achieved at any price.

- **Productivity**. Some companies set productivity goals rather than absolute performance goals. These may be in the form of sales productivity, such as sales per employee or sales per branch, or profit productivity, such as profit per customer or return on sales (or capital employed). These goals ensure that your company is operating efficiently but can be harder to communicate to your people and don't address your absolute levels of performance.

Selecting your metric is a critical discussion for your executive team. As you can see, there are no right or wrong answers. It is your collective judgement about what will best drive the behaviours of your people and the long-term value of your business that should be used to choose your goal. You can then select a handful of counter-balancing goals to ensure that your goal is achieved in the right way and the longer-term interests of your organization.

2.   What level of ambition should you set?

Setting goals is an art as much as a science. The best goals are grounded in an understanding of what is achievable or possible for a business, but include sufficient stretch that new solutions, new growth and new behaviours are required to achieve them. When JFK said that the US should put a man on the moon before the end of the 1960s he did so on an understanding of the technological progress that NASA had already made (i.e. he knew that the goal was certainly possible), but he also knew that his country would need to commit further to make it happen.

Similarly, Jack Welch's goals for GE's business units were certainly feasible and dramatically accelerated the growth of the corporation, but they could not be achieved by simply continuing to do better what the BU's were already doing. The size of the ambition forced the business unit managers to think and act differently. In short, the optimum level of ambition allows you to answer "Yes" to each of these two questions:

- Is this level of performance improvement feasible?
- Does this level of performance demand that we act and behave differently?

3.   What time frame should you set for achieving the goal?

Your final question is how long you want to give yourself and your business to achieve the goal you've set. Here you are balancing the need for pace with recognition of the realities of your existing performance. There is, of course, a link between the time frame you set and the scale of your ambition. Simply put, bigger ambitions take longer to realize. I have found that, for most executive teams, a 3-5 year period gives time to make big changes but is also sufficiently brief that the team know that they must get going immediately and cannot procrastinate for too long (after all, they may well be still around at the end of the goal period). Your ultimate goal can also be broken-down (or extended) by looking at three different periods or horizons:

- Horizon 1: Your organization's performance improvement towards your #1 goal over the next 12-18 months;
- Horizon 2: The level of improvement required over the next three years or so; and
- Horizon 3: The ambition you have for your business in the longer term, say over the next five to ten years.

Whatever time horizon or horizons you use, the key, of course, is to commit to delivering against the goal you set.

At *ServiceExcel* the executive team had several potential #1 goals, including total profits, total sales, market share, number of stores, number of customers and customer satisfaction and loyalty. After an in-depth discussion they realised that the number of customers was the key driver of the company's economic model. As long as the team counter-balanced that goal with some supporting goals around conversion and customer satisfaction, by increasing the number of customers management realized that sales, market share and profit would look after themselves. The company set itself a public goal of 25% improvement within 3 years, although privately the team was committed to growth of 50%.

The beauty of this goal was that it was easy to grasp at the front line. It could be broken down into individual branch goals so that branch and area managers could focus their teams onto what was most important.

Are you drowning in data and suffering from an excessive number of conflicting objectives? Or have you identified your #1 goal and focused your organisation on delivering it in the right way?

Where You Will Play

This element of the strategy statement sets out the scope of your business; the technical term for it is your *participation strategy*. You can radically change the success of your business by re-focusing its scope and choosing a new playing field to play on. Apple, for example, has transformed its performance and the markets it operates in by re-defining its product markets from personal computers to personal electronic devices. By realising that its technology and design capabilities were not limited to PC's the company has become a world leader in music, entertainment and mobile phones.

In the previous chapter I made the point, under strategy's Fatal Flaw #2, that too many companies use incremental rather than step-change thinking. Clarifying your playing field or business scope is a valuable tool to break away from your incremental approaches and to revisit your business with fresh eyes. Famously, Andrew Grove, the former CEO of Intel, asked himself in the 1980s what a new management team would do with his company. His answer was that any new team would move out of its main business of memory chips, where it was becoming disadvantaged against its far east competitors, and make more of its secondary business, microprocessors. So, that is just what Grove and his team did, turning around the fortunes of the business and establishing Intel as one of Silicon Valley's major players.

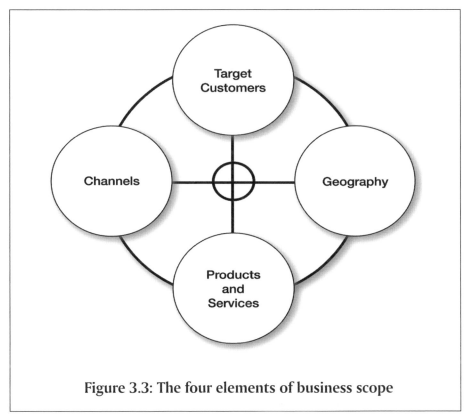

Figure 3.3: The four elements of business scope

Figure 3.3 summarises the four elements of your business scope; your playing field. These elements are:

1. **Target customers**. Key questions to answer include:
   - Who are your ideal customers and how would you describe them?

- If you can meet and exceed the needs of these customers' will you deliver the performance goals you have set for your business?
- Are there other customer groups you can profitably target that you have currently missed or chosen not to serve?
- Are you targeting certain customers that are not profitable and would you be better reducing or removing your focus on them?

2. **Products and services**. Key questions to answer include:
   - What products and services do you offer your target customers?
   - What markets and categories do these products and services cover?
   - Are there related products, services or categories that you could profitably enter into?
   - Are there certain products and services that provide you with low returns, and where you are disadvantaged against your competition, that you should exit?

3. **Channels**. Key questions to answer include:
   - Through which channels do you currently sell and distribute your products and services to your target customers?
   - What other related products and services could you deliver to your customers through these channels?
   - Are there channels that you do not currently use that your target customers would value?
   - Are you using certain channels that are unprofitable and where you are disadvantaged that you should exit?

4. **Geography**. Key questions to answer include:
   - What is your current geographical reach?
   - Are there geographies with similar customers into which you could expand your business profitably?
   - Are there certain regions or countries where you are not competitively advantaged and that you should exit?

Of course, it is difficult to fully answer these questions without undertaking some analysis (which we'll cover in Chapter 4), but unless you and your team are completely new to the business it's likely that you'll have some immediate views and insights that you can use to shape your initial thinking. The other critical aspect of articulating your playing field is that you quickly find that you need to look at the four questions holistically. You may start by answering the individual questions, but you will then need to bring it back together to ensure that the overall scope makes sense. Apple's focus on the *personal* (rather than corporate) element of personal computing, for example, encouraged Steve Jobs and his executive team to expand into other personal electronic products at a time when Microsoft remained focused on its Office software.

At *ServiceExcel*, the CEO realised that the future scope of his business involved a key change. The executive team agreed to define their product and service market more widely. This allowed them to consider future moves into adjacent markets, once they had succeeded in winning a greater share of their target customers.

How You Will Win

The third element of the strategy statement is how and where you will be advantaged against your competitors. Understanding and describing what makes you unique and valued by customers, and enables you to deliver superior performance, provides a focus for ongoing investment and development.

The choice of how you will win depends on three things: what your target customers value most, your organisational capabilities, and how your competitors stack up. Organisations with a clear sense of how they will win and what they will be famouse for enjoy the benefits of focused energy in a way that is simply not present in those companies trying to fight equally on all competitive fronts.

The most liberating, yet most difficult, aspect of strategy development is choosing your key area of differentiation. When asked, *"What kind of business do you want to be? Do you want to have the best products, best service or lowest prices?"* many CEOs simply say *"Yes, we want to be all of those things."* This response is both unrealistic and misguided. It's hard enough to be truly world-class and market-leading on one of these aspects of strategy, never mind all of them. In fact, although there are infinite strategy variations, it is possible to identify these five generic strategies:

1. **Product Leader.** These companies want to have the latest and best products for their target customers. New product development is critical to their success, and customers are willing to pay more to get the high quality product, service or brand experience they're after. Examples include Apple, Sony, Nike and Ferrari.

2. **Cost Leader.** These companies offer amazing prices to their customers who, in turn, believe that the product quality is good enough given the amazingly low prices. Examples include CostCo, Aldi and Primark.

3. **Convenience Leader.** These companies offer a clear standard of performance and deliver against it every time. They are highly dependable, highly convenient and hassle-free. Their strong operational focus and highly efficient systems often mean that they are also low cost organisations. Examples include McDonalds, Toyota, Dell and Amazon.

4. **Service Leader.** These organisations gain and keep clients as a result of the expert advice and customer support they offer, both before and after purchase. Examples include John Lewis, Nordstroms, Home Depot, Lexus and Singapore Airlines.

5. **Solutions Leader.** These businesses tailor their offer to individual customers, creating bespoke solutions. Close and deep relationships with their customers are critical to their success. Examples include McKinsey, IBM and many bespoke engineering firms.

Which organisations can you name that lead on three or four these dimensions? If you can name one or two, congratulations, but these exceptions simply prove the rule. The world's top organisations make clear choices about where and how they wish to differentiate themselves. They focus on one, or possibly two, of these dimensions, and a major reason they do this is that different strategies demand different types of organization. While, for example, a *Product Leader* company, such as Apple or BMW, will emphasise new product development and have many organic cross-functional project teams working on bringing new ideas to market, a *Cost Leader* business, such as Aldi or Tata, will have very simple, centralised processes, and will strictly control costs in all areas of the organisation.

So which strategy should your business be pursuing? The answer is likely to be found by understanding where your organisation's capabilities, the key needs of your market, and your passions meet.

Strategic Focus And customer reactions	Uncompetitive Behind the pack	Competitive In the pack	Distinctive Ahead of the pack	Breakthrough In your own pack
Product Leader "It costs more, but it's worth it"				
Cost Leader "I can't believe the value"				
Convenience Leader "It's all so hassle-free"				
Service Leader "They offer such great advice and support"				
Solutions Leader "It's exactly the solution I was after"				

Figure 3.4: The Strategic Focus Profile

As a first step to setting a direction and agreeing how your organization will win in the future, take these steps, ideally with your team:

- Using Figure 3.4 on the previous page map out the existing strategic profile of your key competitors on each of the five dimensions. Using your own knowledge, customer feedback and their performance data identify whether they are Uncompetitive, Competitive, Advantaged or Breakthrough.

- Now it's your turn. Place a "C" for "Current" in the relevant box for each of the five types of Strategic Focus. Are you behind the pack, in the pack, ahead of the pack, or so good you've created your own pack?

- Next, for each strategic dimension place an "F" for "Future" in the box that you aspire to be over the next 3-5 years. Would you like to improve, and if so how radically, or do you think you should stay the same or perhaps decline in your relative performance on each dimension?

- Finally, review the profile that you've developed. The gap between your current position and your future ambition indicates the level of work you will need to undertake to achieve your goals.

You will of course need to carry out more work to validate the direction you have provisionally set. But what's your initial reaction to the potential future direction of your company? What level of excitement does it give you about the type of organisation you could become? After all, without a sense of excitement, mission and anticipation, it's unlikely that you'll deliver a strategy of any value whatsoever.

After critically reviewing several alternatives the executive team at *ServiceExcel* decided to focus their advantage on their ability to offer personalised solutions to their customers. Although they knew they had to be competitive on price, convenience and product quality, the CEO and his executive team believed that it was the extra element of service and support in choosing the ideal solution that the company could give its customers that would best create a competitive advantage for the business and drive its future growth and profitability.

What You Must Focus On

The final element of *The Strategy Arrow* lists your top 3-6 strategic objectives, the critical themes that you will focus on over the next few years to deliver your #1 goal and turn your strategy into reality. Put simply, it sets out what you need to do to get from where you are now to where you want to be.

The *ServiceExcel* executive team identified five strategic themes to drive their leadership agenda, which it called its 'formula for growth':

- *Great Value Solutions*. The company ensured that there were great products at all price points, recognising that, although the business didn't want to be the cost and price leader, it did need to reduce the gap with some of their competitors.

- *Attracting More Customers*. Specific projects and initiatives were put in place to ensure that more customers were attracted and retained as *ServiceExcel* customers.

- *A Unique Experience*. In line with the company's brand and decision on how the company will win in the future, the team set about creating a seamless customer service experience that delivered personalised solutions.

- *Partnerships For Growth*. The leadership team identified that working with partners gave them the quickest most direct route to growth, and began to create strategic alliances with a focused group of corporate partners.

- *Colleagues who love people.* Recruitment, management and recognition were all focused on developing teams and colleagues who were comfortable and effective in delivering the personalised customer experience.

Putting It All Together

As I have said, your initial ideas and assumptions will need to be tested and verified and, if necessary, amended. However, you will rapidly accelerate the speed at which you develop your strategy if you start the process with a view of the final strategy. You may find that you need to develop two or three alternative strategies. That too is fine as you can then focus your subsequent analysis on testing your thinking rather than simply undertaking analysis and research for the sake of it. Of course, it is critical, even after you have set out your initial views, to keep an open mind and to let the facts speak for themselves. The strategy development process is a time for open thinking and looking at options. If you close your thinking and mind too early, you may find that you haven't been sufficiently radical or objective.

Here's how the team at *ServiceExcel* pulled the four elements of into a coherent and simple statement.

> *Our goal **over the next three years** is to serve **1 million customers** by providing **convenient and personalised solutions** across **the UK** to **working women and their families**, delivered through our **national branch network** and our **on-line reach.***
>
> *To make this a reality we are focused on five strategic objectives:*
>
> *1. Great Value Solutions*
>
> *2. Attract More Customers*
>
> *3. Deliver A Unique Experience*
>
> *4. Partnerships For Growth*
>
> *5. Colleagues Who Love People*

This statement provided the CEO and his team with the clarity needed to help the wider organisation of healthcare professionals, consultants and support colleagues understand, buy into and deliver the strategy. Behind each of the words has been intense debate and analysis, but that enables all of the executive team to tell the same story time and time again.

Key Points

- The strategy process benefits by starting with the end in mind and setting out an initial strategy hypothesis
- A vision is not a strategy, and you are likely to spend your time more productively if you create a clear strategy that talks about how you intend to succeed in the future
- There are four elements to a business strategy – an unambiguous statement of your #1 goal, a description of your future business scope and where you will play, an assessment of where you will be advantaged and how you will win, and a focused set of medium-term objectives for your organization to pursue
- Your #1 goal should both be feasible and ensure that you need to behave and act differently to achieve it – you shouldn't be able to get there just by doing 'more of the same'
- Your business scope and your playing field has four dimensions – target customers; products and services; channels; and geographies
- When deciding how you will win you need to determine which of these five strategies you wish to pursue – product leadership; cost leadership; convenience leadership; service leadership; solutions leadership
- You should set your organization 3-6 objectives to focus on to deliver your strategy
- Once you have verified your strategy you should create a focused and pithy strategy statement that you can use to communicate the direction of your business with the rest of your organization and your wider stakeholders

Chapter 4

WHERE ON EARTH ARE YOU HEADING?

A Little Analysis Can Go A Long Way; A Lot Of Analysis Can Quickly Get You Lost!

One of the reasons why many successful executives prefer not to get involved in developing strategies for their business is that they believe it involves unnecessary navel-gazing. These managers would much prefer to be getting on with their 'real jobs' than carrying out endless analysis and form-filling. To be honest, I have a lot of sympathy with their views. Too much effort on strategy is placed on analysis, and too much analysis is unfocused and far from insightful. Done well, however, analysis can be used to challenge your 'gut feel' and give you the confidence to deliver more radical and customer-focused change to your business. This means that the analysis should be sufficiently robust to ensure that you gain agreement across your executive team about your current position and direction, without dragging you into some kind of spreadsheet nightmare or the creation of a myriad of reports that will never be read.

Oh No, Not Another SWOT!

A friend of mine once told me that SWOT stood for 'Stupid Waste Of Time'. He has a point, and yet *"Let's do a SWOT"* is a common response to the suggestion of understanding a company's strategic position. Just in case you don't know – and for everyone else, please feel free to skip this paragraph – SWOT actually stands for

Strengths, Weaknesses, Opportunities and Threats. The SWOT framework became popular across companies in the 1960s and 1970s as a way of building an agenda for action. In short, companies grow by building their strengths, addressing their weaknesses, exploiting their key opportunities and acting to prevent and mitigate potential threats.

So far, so logical. But there are three key reasons why SWOT analyses are unhelpful:

1. **They are long lists, not focused insights**. Most SWOT analyses end up as a long, unprioritized list. Even if you were to accept that each item, on its own, was valid, there is no way that any organization can act on 20 or 30 issues simultaneously. Completing the lists may feel cleansing and cathartic to executive teams, but it does little to set up the team for action.

2. **They are based on opinion, not facts**. Opinions are important in strategy development. They create breakthroughs and innovations that drive businesses forward. But without a certain level of rigour to back up these opinions they may lead you up a blind alley. I once worked with a UK supermarket chain that had decided that it should invest in improving staff satisfaction across their store chain, believing that by doing so customer satisfaction, loyalty and spend would grow. Unfortunately, when I researched what was important to customers, employee satisfaction or even engaging with staff wasn't that important. Instead, customers wanted lower prices and better stock availability. It came as something of a shock to the management team to find out that the stores with the highest levels of customer satisfaction also had the lowest staff satisfaction, and that their investment in the HR programme would have been better spent on reducing prices.

3. **They can miss key issues**. As with the grocer example above, the focus on brainstormed and unchecked lists can mean that the real issues are not identified or addressed. Sometimes these issues are obvious, at least in hindsight. But in other cases, you only identify the issue by undertaking some focused analysis. For example, I helped a $50 million healthcare business identify new opportunities for growth, and, as part of the project, assessed the relative rates of return the business was getting through its various sales channels. It was only when we critically looked at these returns that it became obvious that the pharmacy

channel sales' teams were less profitable than other channels sales' teams, and that we needed to consider alternative ways of selling to pharmacies that would give the company a better return.

Analysis of your organization and its performance does not have to involve wading in piles of data. It should be focused, targeted and specific. There are three critical factors you must consider:

1. **Work at the right level in the business.** Not all analysis should take place at the whole company level, and segmenting your business is a great way to identify key insights and issues. When I ran the strategy team for UK retailer, Boots the Chemists, we performed some analysis at a company level, but most was at a level or two below this. For example, in terms of product strategy, we would focus on category level analysis (e.g. pharmacy category, cosmetics category, toiletries category), and for store performance we would identify issues by looking through regional and format lenses. Before you begin any analysis, you should therefore ask yourself what level in the business structure is likely to give you meaningful results.

2. **Answer specific questions and hypotheses.** A big problem with the large consulting firms is that they undertake excessive analysis with no end in mind. You will get far better results if you limit your work to answering specific questions you have. Even better, as we shall see, starting off with an opinion or idea – call them hypotheses to sound more authoritative! – will help give you laser-like focus on the work that is required.

3. **Develop actionable insights**. As the name suggests, an 'actionable insight' is one that enables you to do something as a result of understanding it. For example, finding out that you pay key staff 30% below market rates is an actionable insight; discovering that 10% of purchases made by your most loyal customers on a Wednesday have an average 4.7 items in the basket, but that this drops to 3.6 items on a Thursday, is not an actionable insight. Analysts can easily get lost in the detail when they undertake this work. Once, when I was trying to find the right product offer for a group of stores a colleague turned to me and said, *"Stuart you're not drowning in data, you're bog-snorkelling in it!"* You must lift your analysts out of the bog so that they deliver insights you can do something about.

Focusing Your Analysis On Things That Matter

One of the aspects of strategy development that puts many executives off is the amount of data analysis that seems to accompany it. In most cases, however, this 'boil the ocean' approach simply adds to the level of work rather than to the level of insight or the quality of the final decision.

The good news is that strategy development doesn't have to work that way.

When it comes to strategy development you need neither to 'boil the ocean' trying to find the perfect solution or simply go with your 'gut feel'. Focusing your analysis on your key hypotheses will help you make informed decisions with pace and confidence. When I work with my clients I find I can increase the speed and effectiveness of the work by focusing first on the executive team's opinions. We call these hypotheses or assumptions, but the premise is the same: if we start with an answer we usually get to a better solution faster, even if it is different to the one we started with. The process I use is summarised in the chart set out in Figure 4.1, the '4A Framework'.

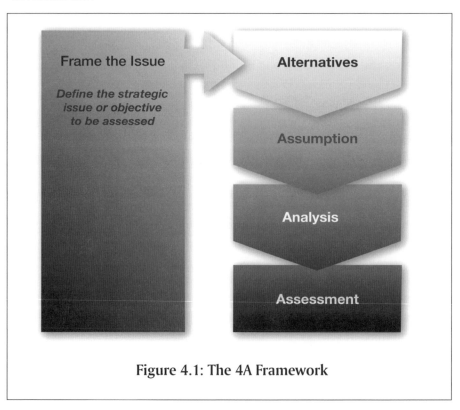

Figure 4.1: The 4A Framework

Whatever issue you are seeking to resolve the process you follow is the same:

1. **Frame The Issue**. You do not tend to carry out an engineering survey of your home without first having a question you're trying to answer. Yet, many strategy processes undertake analysis without any reference to specific questions. Before you begin your analysis sit down with your team and identify a list of specific issues and opportunities that you wish to better understand and resolve, and agree some specific questions. The issue may be as general as *"How can we best grow profits in our markets?"* or may be more specific and pointed, for example *"How can we reduce our unit costs of production?"*

2. **Alternatives**. Your next step is to set out what your broad alternatives are. Taking the question of growing profits you may quickly sketch out four alternatives: (1) Grow sales volumes, (2) Raise prices, (3) Reduce production costs, or (4) Reduce business overheads.

3. **Assumption**. In order to focus your analysis, you should then take a view as to which alternative (or combination of alternatives) is likely to offer the best solution. Using the example, you may make an initial decision that the first alternative, growing sales volumes, is your preferred way forward. You may know that there are still many customers you haven't reached and there are sectors of the market you don't currently serve. You may also have evidence that it is not possible to raise prices, that the best way to reduce unit production costs is to drive up volumes anyway, and that your overheads are too small to make a material impact on profit performance.

4. **Analysis**. The critical difference between a strategy based on hope and one based on insight is the quality of the supporting analysis. The next step is therefore to ask yourself what needs to be true for you to be able to grow volumes by reaching new customers and entering new sectors of the market. Be specific. What is that you must achieve if you are to succeed, and what evidence can you obtain – from research, trials or performance data – that they are within your reach?

5. **Assessment**. The final stage is to make an informed choice based on the analysis you've undertaken, balancing risk and return. If your first hypothesis does not appear to be as attractive as you first thought, you will need to consider one or more of the other alternatives, but at least you have not simply 'boiled the ocean' in a search for any answer.

From The Top: Stephen Ford

Stephen Ford is the President and General Manager of Avon Cosmetics, Australia and New Zealand. Having a background in strategy, including VP of Strategy for Avon in Europe and Africa, this is his first full operational role for this iconic cosmetics brand.

The core thread that has run throughout my career has been the development of company strategies, both as a management consultant and as a leader within businesses. So I recognise the importance of having a clear, focused strategy for a business, helping people across the organization pull in the same direction and understand where the company is heading. Since taking over as the President for Avon's Australia and New Zealand business, I have learnt three critical lessons.

First, it is paramount that the leader makes the strategy tangible. I cannot let the strategy be seen as an abstract idea that has no relevance to everyone's day-to-day activities, otherwise it will die. Consequently, my first strategic decision was to set a clear, stretching performance goal for the business. Having looked at various options with my executive team, we settled on a goal of receiving 1 million orders from our tens of thousands of representatives. We chose this goal because, all things being equal, growing orders will drive our profitability. But we also used this goal as it's memorable – everyone can remember the "1 million orders" target. As a result, we have energized the wider organization and also use the scale of growth we're after as a benchmark to decide which projects to pursue and which to park.

The second lesson I've learned is that we must focus on the big stuff, and not get distracted by less important matters. There are many areas where our business could improve, but if we tried to sort all our issues our organization would simply seize up. We must deliver our current performance goals and service standards as we deliver our new strategy, and so we pick our operational battles carefully, and only make changes where the prize and strategic gains are worth it. As a VP of Strategy I could create a long list of areas for improvement, but as the country president I have learned to say "no" to many opportunities, so that we can ensure we are successful with our critical strategic projects.

Finally, my third lesson has been the importance of asking provocative questions, rather than relying on detailed analyses to drive our strategy discussions. We are a lean team and so, while we need enough facts to ensure our conversations are robust, I recognise the need to trust the judgement and wisdom of my team. The way to bring that wisdom out onto the table has been my ability to ask challenging questions. I have also leveraged my role as the country's boss to get direct feedback and ideas from the front line, and use their insights to challenge my executive team, something that representatives would be far less willing to share with me when I was in a strategy role.

The Four Strategy Perspectives

You cannot reach any destination if you don't understand your current position. Getting a handle on your market position and your current performance, together with a view of your most likely future growth and profitability, will help you determine the key steps you need to take in order to make your goals and objectives a reality. You must understand your existing strategic position, and assess the future direction of your business under its current strategy.

As set out in the Figure 4.2, there are four elements of a robust strategic assessment. Although strong financial results are the litmus test of success, they are driven by the development of capable organizations, strong competitive positions, and by participation in attractive markets. Assessing your business from each of these four perspectives will give you a rounded view of your ability to hit your goals. If you use the 4A framework alongside the analytical approaches I set out below you will also answer the specific questions you have around your future growth strategy.

Figure 4.2: The Four Strategy Perspectives

1.   Financial Performance

There are five steps to creating an insightful assessment of your financial performance.

1. **Break down your business into discrete business segments**
   A business is not typically a homogenous entity, but comprises several businesses. Many businesses are broken down into divisions or business units, but even when this isn't the case you should still take the time to identify discrete business segments. You need to shine a torch on all of your business activities, and, this way, you will get a handle on the performance – at a financial, organizational, competitive and market level – of your entire business, and will avoid success in one area concealing weaknesses elsewhere.

As you do this work, you may be surprised how many business segments you really operate. At this stage, err on the side of over-segmentation – you can always combine segments at a later stage – and create a new segment where:

- ▶ The products or services you offer are distinctively different; or
- ▶ The competitors you face are different; or
- ▶ The customers you serve are different.

2. **Identify sales for each segment over the past three years**
   Using available information from your records, determine the sales and the level of growth, over the past three years. In some areas, it may be straightforward to get the information, but where you have identified business segments that you haven't historically recorded separately, you may need to estimate some of the sales, at least. If possible, you should separate out gross sales from discounts given in each of the segments.

   Why use three years of data? Well, a three-year view enables you to start to identify performance trends, rather than recent one-off events, but is a short enough period of time that allows most management teams to collect reasonably robust data. But, if you only have a year or two's worth of usable data, you should still be able to generate new business insights.

3. **Identify the costs for each business segment for the past three years**
   At this stage you are looking to divide the costs into three types:
   - ▶ *Costs of Sale.* These are the costs required to manufacture the product or deliver the service, including the costs of bought-in materials and production.
   - ▶ *Sales, Marketing, Development and Distribution Costs.* These are the costs directly associated with bringing the product or service to market for your customers. They include the cost of the sales, marketing and development teams, advertising, sponsorship, R&D, distribution and post-production storage.
   - ▶ *General and Administrative Costs.* These are the costs that are not directly attributable to developing, producing, selling or distributing your products and services. Typically, they include the cost of senior management and the finance, HR, IT and legal functions.

The purpose of collecting this information is to allocate the costs across your discrete business segments. Most businesses are able to allocate the cost of raw and bought-in materials, and even track costs of production by different product groups.

It is less common to allocate sales, marketing and administrative costs directly across your business segments. As a result, the process will involve some estimates and high-level judgements. The simplest approach is to allocate the costs on the basis of sales turnover, but we all know that some areas of the business are more costly to run than others.

As a result, you should allocate each major element of cost on its most appropriate basis. For example:

▶ The cost of sales teams could be allocated by the time the teams spend on different products and accounts;

▶ Development costs should be split by the time spent by the teams on specific projects, as well as the direct costs of creating new products and services; and

▶ Production costs could be determined by the time of different product groups spent on specific production lines.

Ask each of your relevant senior managers to develop their own recommendation for cost allocation to ensure that the resulting analysis is robust and owned across the organization.

4. **Do the same for your capital employed**
   Use the same approach to allocate your capital employed across your discrete business segments. Capital employed comprises two elements: fixed capital, such as plant and equipment, vehicles, buildings and IT systems; and working capital, which is the sum of your stock (finished goods, work in progress and raw materials) and your outstanding sales invoices, less the value of your accounts payable.

5. **Complete the Financial Performance chart and identify key insights**
   The final stage is to pull together the data and identify the insights that could help you dramatically improve the performance of your business. Figure 4.3 gives you a one-page summary of the data (of a fictional retail chain) that will allow you to identify key issues and opportunities.

Pinfolds Retail Chain Financial Summary	Business Segment			Company Total
	Cycle Shops	Ski Shops	Surf Shops	
Sales	200	150	125	475
Gross Profit	80	70	55	205
Sales, Marketing & Distribution Costs	(60)	(50)	(40)	(150)
General & Administrative Costs	(15)	(11)	(12)	(38)
Operating Profit	5	9	3	17
3-Year Sales Growth %	2.5%	8.5%	15.0%	7.7%
3-Year Profit Growth %	4.5%	12.0%	7.5%	9.0%
Working Capital	35	25	20	80
Fixed Capital	65	45	35	145
Total Capital Employed	100	70	55	225
Gross Margin %	40%	47%	44%	43%
Operating Margin %	2.5%	6.0%	2.0%	3.6%
Return on Capital Employed %	5.0%	12.9%	5.5%	7.6%

Figure 4.3: Financial Performance Assessment

As you review the outputs, you should look to answer these questions:

▶ Where are we making money and where are we losing it?
▶ Where is our business growing and where are we stagnating or going backwards?
▶ Where are we making acceptable levels of return on capital employed and where are we falling short?

2. Organizational Capabilities

Your future success is dependent on the quality and vibrancy of your organization. If you under-invest in developing your company's capabilities, you may find that your results and competitive position can quickly decline. The quality of your organization's capabilities is a function of the strength of your underlying assets and skills, the retention and attitude of your people and the quality of your leadership. The key to success is matching your capabilities to the needs of your target customers in such a way that your competitors find it hard to match.

Determining your key capabilities

Many executive teams take the time to list out their organization's key capabilities. Often, however, this can be based on hubris rather than reality. Just because you have one recent product launch that is growing share does not necessarily make product innovation one of your key capabilities. There are three factors that determine the strength of your key capabilities:

- ■ *They are instrumental in driving material success for your organization.* Your key capabilities are critical to your current success and should be capable of helping to launch you into new market opportunities. Sony's imaging, digital and optical capabilities has not only delivered success in its core home entertainment categories, but has enabled it to expand into other markets, such as personal computers, cameras and video equipment.

- ■ *They are difficult for others to copy.* If others can quickly and easily copy what you're great at, you won't have a competitive advantage for long. One of the reasons why competitors have historically found it hard to match the personal service offered by Ritz Carlton's hotel chain is that it is the company's key focus and is built on a specific organizational culture and management approach. Other hotel chains are unable or simply unwilling to make the trade-offs necessary to deliver the quality of service that Ritz Carlton achieves.

- ■ *They are a combination of factors, not a single skill.* It is far harder for other organizations to replicate your success if your capabilities are a tightly woven mix of skills rather than a unique, specific area of expertise. Wal-Mart, for example, has not become the world's biggest retailer, offering all the key brands at low prices, simply because the company's managers have effective buying negotiation skills. It has succeeded, in part, because it has invested in market-leading systems and processes that enable suppliers to manage inventory on behalf of the grocer, dramatically reducing Wal-Mart's operating costs and working capital requirements. Wal-Mart's capability in 'integrated inventory management' combines skills in IT development, logistics management, negotiation skills and forecasting.

So how do you get beyond the obvious lists of assumed strengths to a deeper understand of what really makes your company succeed? I propose that 5 simple questions can provide you with meaningful insights that will help guide your company's future strategic direction.

1. **Which of our products/services are outperforming the market and generating superior returns?**
   Understanding which product/service categories outperform the market is your first clue as to what makes your company successful. Where are you experiencing high sales and profit growth? Where do you have high market shares, and where are these growing? Where do you have high margins and where are these greater than the market? Importantly, the areas where you are winning may not necessarily be where your sales are highest! You need to look for unusual and unexpected areas of success, and these may be tucked away in some of your smaller business areas.

2. **What are the characteristics of these products/services?**
   The second question enables you to identify common characteristics of your leading product and service categories. Are they new product ranges or old? Do they require high levels of pre/after sales service, or are they self-select? Are they exclusive or freely competed? Are you able to offer a premium price, or have you discounted to the market? You should look for trends and patterns that suggest a common cause.

3. **Which customers are buying these products/services?**
   In most cases you will not be winning with all customers, but with certain customer groups. Understanding which customers are driving your growth and profit is critical to understanding what makes you successful. What are the demographic (who are they?) and psychographic (what makes them tick?) characteristics of these buyers?

4. **What do we know about the specific reasons these customers buy these products/services from us?**
   Ideally you will have some reliable customer research, otherwise you need to get as close to the customer as possible. Talking to your sales teams will give you a good indication of the reasons if you probe appropriately. Importantly, it's not always about price. I worked with a household products' manufacturer where we identified that product quality and product availability were the 'order winning' factors, and that price was, for most customers, a hygiene factor. It was important to be competitive on price, but simply lowering prices wouldn't drive gains in share if the quality and availability issues weren't addressed.

5. **What are the capabilities, and underlying skills, that have enabled us to deliver these results?**

Once you understand why customers buy from you, it is a short step to identifying your key skills and capabilities. For the household products' manufacturer, product development capabilities, inventory management and responsive distribution became the key capabilities on which the company's future success was based.

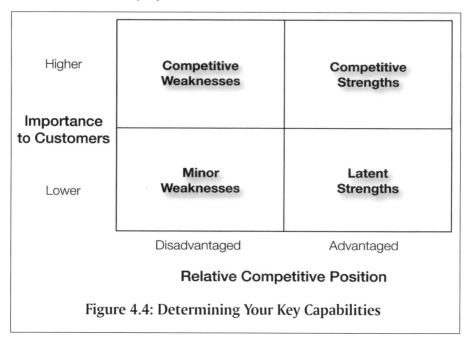

Figure 4.4: Determining Your Key Capabilities

Collating the answers to these five questions will give you a useful tool for understanding what makes your company successful. Investing where you are strong and have further potential - and, conversely, taking cost and investment out of the business where you are disadvantaged – is the key to corporate success. As you review these factors, using the framework set our in Figure 4.4, you should answer the following questions:

- What are the skills, capabilities and assets that help your company succeed and stand out from your competitors?
- Are these capabilities becoming more or less important to your customers, and stronger or weaker relative to your competitors?
- How well are you able to retain the people that are most important to delivering these skills and capabilities?

3. Competitive Position

In general, strong financial performance is based on your ability to turn your organization's capabilities into distinctive competitive advantages. So, how do you know if you are advantaged? Well, there are some tell-tale signs:

- You are gaining market share;
- Your profit margins are higher than your competitors;
- Your customer satisfaction and loyalty is higher than your competitors;
- You are able to justify a price premium;
- Your brand is perceived as being stronger and more attractive than your competitors.

Using our fictional retail chain and its key competitors as an example, figure 4.5 provides a one-page summary of these factors that you can use to assess the strength of your competitive positions across your different markets and business segments. Completing the chart requires you to have a reasonable understanding of both your customers' perceptions and your competitors' performance. You may or may not have immediate access to these pieces of information. Where you are unable or unwilling to undertake more detailed research, you should work with a cross-section of managers to generate your organization's best view. Gaining a variety of opinions – covering the front line as well as top management – is likely to reduce the personal bias that you and your fellow executive directors may possess.

Here are some pointers to help you complete the chart:

- Use the same business segments that you've developed for your financial performance assessment;
- 3-Year CAGR stands for Compound Annual Growth Rate and is the average annual percentage sales growth you have achieved over the past three years;
- Ensure that, as near as possible, you use the same definition of profit across each of the players in your market;
- You should ensure that you have captured your top competitors for each of your business segments. Of course, not every competitor will be present in all your business segments.

Pinfolds vs Key Competitors Sales Peformance $m	Business Segment			Company Total	Ave. 3-Yr Sales Growth %	Ave. 3-Yr Sales Growth %
	Cycle Shops	Ski Shops	Surf Shops			
Pinfold's	200	150	125	475	7.7%	3.5%
Lowman	500			500	12.5%	7.5%
Track & Field	250	100		350	4.6%	6.5%
Sports Mad	250	100	50	400	7.2%	5.4%
Mountain & Sea		75	150	225	2.5%	4.7%
Snow & Surf		75	25	100	1.6%	3.1%
Surfman			50	50	6.0%	10.0%
Others	800	500	350	1,650	2.0%	
Total Segment Size	2,000	1,000	750	3,750	5.0%	

Figure 4.5a Assessing Your Competitive Position

Pinfolds vs Key Competitors
Customer Ratings

Top 5 Customer Needs- *Rating Out of 10*

Cycle Shops

Customer Need	1 Quality	2 Range	3 Price	4 Service	5 Convenience
Pinfolds	6.0	7.5	6.5	8.0	7.0
Lowman	8.5	8.0	7.0	7.0	9.5
Track & Field	7.5	7.0	7.0	6.0	5.0
Sports Mad	7.0	6.0	8.0	7.5	6.5

Ski Shops

Customer Need	1 Service	2 Range	3 Quality	4 Price	5 Offers
Pinfolds	9.5	8.5	8.0	7.0	7.5
Track & Field	8.0	7.0	7.5	7.0	8.0
Sports Mad	8.5	8.0	7.0	7.5	8.0
Mountain & Sea	7.0	5.0	6.0	7.5	7.5
Snow & Surf	7.5	7.0	7.0	6.0	6.5

Surf Shops

Customer Need	1 Range	2 Price	3 Quality	4 Offers	5 Service
Pinfolds	7.0	9.0	7.5	8.5	7.0
Track & Field	7.5	7.0	8.0	7.0	7.5
Sports Mad	7.5	7.0	8.5	8.0	8.0
Mountain & Sea	7.0	7.0	8.0	6.5	8.0
Snow & Surf	6.5	6.5	8.5	7.5	8.0
Surfman	8.0	8.0	8.5	7.5	8.0

In the example, *Pinfolds* has three retail formats and business segments covering bicycle shops, ski clothing and equipment, and surfing equipment and accessories. The analysis highlights the following insights:

- *Lowman* is growing rapidly in the bicycle retail sector, driven by a combination of high product quality and convenience. *Pinfolds* is at #4 in this market and its share is going backwards due to the lower perceived product quality of its bikes.
- *Pinfolds* is the market leader in ski clothing and equipment and is particularly advantaged in its quality of service.
- *Pinfolds* has the second largest share in the surfing retail market but its profit margins are significantly behind its competitors. It appears that it is growing through its lower prices, but that others are making more money.

As you identify these insights you immediately begin to ask yourself questions about how the management of Pinfolds can address its key issues and what the executives should do to maximise the results from their opportunities. The same will happen when you undertake your own analysis. As you review your results, you should answer these questions:

- How well do your target and key customers rate your business and brand (vs. your competitors') on their key needs and preferences?
- What share of the market do you have, and, if you are the market leader, is your position strong enough to give you cost or price advantages?
- What profit margins are you achieving and are these ahead of, or behind, those achieved by your competitors.

4.   Market Attractiveness

Finally you should ask yourself whether the markets you operate in are good businesses to be in, and whether the attractiveness of your markets are likely to improve or worsen in the future. A rising tide floats all boats, and participating in attractive markets makes it easier for businesses to deliver strong returns. Be careful, however. It is more likely that you will deliver profits if you are advantaged in a poor market than it is if you are disadvantaged in an attractive market.

For example, the car industry has, for the past decade or two, been a fairly unattractive business in which to operate. Gigantic fixed costs, rising material costs, and increasing international competition has meant that most automotive players have struggled to deliver strong returns. That said, companies including Nissan and Toyota have been able to cut costs, deliver innovation and drive profits and shareholder returns.

Attractiveness Indicator	Highly Unattractive	Unattractive	Attractive	Highly Attractive
1. What is the average Return On Capital Employed (ROCE) over the last 5 years?	<5%	5-10%	10-20%	>20%
2. What is the ROCE trend?	Falling	Erratic	Stable	Growing
3. What's the likely average volume growth in the market over the next 5 years?	Decline	0-5%	5-10%	>10%
4. How high are the barriers for new entrants?	Very low	Quite low	Quite high	Very high
5. How strong is the competition?	Dominated by World Class players with strong positions	Strong competition with little change in market positions	Reasonable competitor strength but no strong players	Relatively weak and/or complacent competitors
6. What's the balance between demand and supply in the market?	Serious overcapacity	Overcapacity but will be reduced	Quite well balanced	Demand outstrips supply
7. What's the threat from substitute products?	Serious threat	Uncertain	Minor	Unlikely
8. What's your relative bargaining power with your suppliers?	Much weaker	Slightly weaker	Slightly stronger	Much stronger
9. What's your relative bargaining power with your customers?	Much weaker	Slightly weaker	Slightly stronger	Much stronger
10. What's the threat from greater government regulation?	Very High	Quite High	Quite Low	Very Low

Figure 4.6: Assessing Market Attractiveness

Conversely, many personal consumer goods markets, such as dental products, shampoos and conditioners and over-the-counter medicines have grown strongly, remained relatively profitable and enabled many of the players in these markets to deliver reasonable returns. The ageing population, the increased number of single households and the rapid growth in emerging markets has ensured that there has been strong ongoing demand in these sectors.

Many companies spend significant amounts of time and money understanding the attractiveness of their markets. However, you can get a quick and robust view a lot quicker. Figure 4.6 provides you with a straightforward proforma to use for each of the markets in which you operate. Simply decide which of the four responses best answers each of the 10 questions.

After completing the exercise, review the pattern of answers and determine how you would rate each market overall. More importantly, understand why you have rated your market the way you have. Specific questions to answer include:

- Is your market profitable, and can an average player make a reasonable return?
- Is your market large or small, and is it growing, stagnating or declining?
- What are the threats to the future of your market from new technologies, new entrants or substitute markets for your customers?

Identifying Your Big Issues And Opportunities

The purpose of undertaking an assessment of financial performance, organizational health, competitive position and market attractiveness is to identify the key issues and major opportunities you should focus on to achieve your strategic ambitions. You do not undertake the work to delude yourself into believing that everything is OK, even when everyone knows the wheels are starting to come off the car. Equally, you do not carry out the analysis to needlessly beat yourself up when, to continue the car analogy, you should be putting your pedal to the metal.

The success of the review of your business across the four strategy perspectives is, in the end, down to your ability to take an objective, sober view of performance. Critically, the numbers-based analysis is just part of the equation. You should be balancing what the numbers tell you with what you find on the ground. Spending time with your customers and people on the front line is essential to understanding what's really happening in your markets; the analysis should act as confirmation of your hunches and give you an idea of the scale and importance of the issues and opportunities.

Strategy Perspective	Critical Issues	Major Opportunities
Financial Performance	1. _____ 2. _____ 3. _____	1. _____ 2. _____ 3. _____
Organizational Health	1. _____ 2. _____ 3. _____	1. _____ 2. _____ 3. _____
Competitive Position	1. _____ 2. _____ 3. _____	1. _____ 2. _____ 3. _____
Market Attractiveness	1. _____ 2. _____ 3. _____	1. _____ 2. _____ 3. _____

Figure 4.7: Summarizing Your Big Issues And Opportunities

So what does the analysis tell you? Using the chart in Figure 4.7, identify the top three issues and top three opportunities emerging from each of the four strategy perspectives. Think carefully about which are the most important and, if they were to be robustly addressed, would best drive your performance over the next few years and deliver your strategic objectives. Set out a short-list of five or six issues you believe the business should focus on. For example, when I worked with the division of a household product company, the CEO and his team agreed that there were five critical issues and opportunities facing the business:

1. How to better exploit and grow performance in the DIY retail channel\

2. How to drive the quantity and quality of new product development

3. How to radically reduce operating costs

4. How to improve the capabilities and performance of the sales team

5. How to enter new, adjacent product categories

Key Points

- Many executives are put off undertaking strategy projects by the seemingly endless analysis that accompanies it
- A SWOT analysis is not a useful tool to generate real insights on your current position or future trends
- You should focus your analysis on your big questions, rather than taking a scatter-gun approach
- Strategy analysis is best done through four perspectives – Financial Performance, Organizational Health, Competitive Position and Market Attractiveness
- The output of your strategic analysis should be a short-list of the major issues and opportunities that management should focus on to achieve the goals you have set for the business

Chapter 5
NOTHING FAILS LIKE SUCCESS

Why You Must Always Be Focused On Driving Growth

The Perils Of Success

Many companies struggle and fail, not because they are bad at what they do, but because they are great at what they do. Look at Kodak, for example. Its decline hasn't resulted from the company being poor at film processing. On the contrary, the company's success has stalled precisely because it is great at film processing. And it's the same with many other companies. Olivetti, for example, is great at making typewriters, and The Gap is great at making and marketing chinos.

The problem that these and many other competent companies have faced is that things change; markets change, the economy changes, technology changes and customer tastes change. But many companies cannot change their offer or their organization as quickly as their external environment changes. Companies that are able to align their capabilities and build distinctive advantages to perfectly meet current market opportunities cannot necessarily adapt to meet tomorrow's.

There are three reasons for this:

1. **Arrogance**. The US car industry, for example, for many years rejected the idea that the Japanese manufacturers, led by Toyota and Honda, could threaten their domination of their domestic market. They're not saying that now!

2. **Defensiveness**. When the technology first became available, the music industry tried to kill all digital download companies. Instead,

they wanted to protect the sales of the more profitable, older CD technology. One estimate suggests that this has meant that in 2010 the music retail market was worth $15 billion less than it might have been.

3. **Inertia**. This is probably the biggest barrier to change. Many traditional airlines have found it difficult to change their organization in response to the rise of the low fare airlines. It's not a question of arrogance or defensiveness, but simply the investment and time it takes to change the way a large business works.

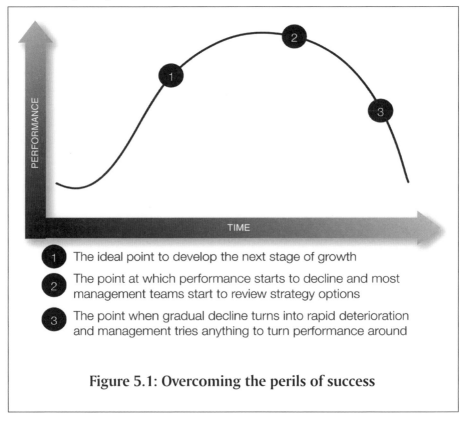

1 The ideal point to develop the next stage of growth

2 The point at which performance starts to decline and most management teams start to review strategy options

3 The point when gradual decline turns into rapid deterioration and management tries anything to turn performance around

Figure 5.1: Overcoming the perils of success

Figure 5.1 sets out a typical profile of a successful company's performance. As it finds a successful formula it begins to achieve success and performance improves rapidly.

■ Position (1) is the ideal point to develop and drive the company's next generation of success, but in most cases management's desire to maintain the current levels of success overrides any latent aspiration to develop a new strategy.

- Position (2) is the period in which performance starts to plateau and slowly decline. Although some organizations use this period to find and pursue a new strategy for success, many continue with their existing strategy and simply take costs out of the business or extend their product and service range in an attempt to boost performance.

- Position (3) is when the slow decline turns to rapid deterioration. At this point most organizations will then try something – anything! –new, but the risks of failure are now so large, it is more likely that the business will fail.

So what can you do about it? How can you help your organization focus on re-setting strategy at position (1) rather than position (3)? Here are four steps you can take:

1. **Look for the weak signals**. If you wait until your profits are being affected, chances are it will be too late. Instead, you need to look at other metrics – your level of NPD, what your more innovative customers are doing, what your brand research tells you. Companies need to be more attuned to these early warning signs. As former Intel boss Andy Grove put it, "*Only the paranoid survive*".

2. **Raise the bar continually**. All market leaders need to set increasing standards for success or their competitors will do it for them. In 2003, for example, the England rugby team won the World Cup. However, by focusing on victory at that tournament as the ultimate goal for the team, it was difficult for the new management to subsequently raise the bar and the team's performance quickly declined.

3. **Focus on action**. If you're moving and acting, you are less likely to get stuck or create inertia. This may involve some failure along the way, but as *Business Week*'s survey of the world's best innovators discovered, the number one factor that drove their success was the ability to "*experiment fearlessly*".

4. **Intelligently cannibalize your own sales**. In a dynamic market, if you don't cannibalize your sales your competitors will do it for you. Apple has brilliantly overcome this issue in the way it has managed the iPod. After its initial launch in 2001 Apple has limited the headroom for competitors to launch rival products by regularly bringing to market new versions of the iPod that deliver better performance at lower prices.

Raising The Bar Continuously

Strategic advances are made when organizations become the first to find a profitable way to exploit new opportunities. These opportunities may be created by changes in customer tastes, technology, economics or other external factors. Critically, strategic advances are not made through problem solving. Resolving problems is about dealing with the past, not the future. Problem solving may help you drive performance – or at least return it to previous levels – but it will not dramatically improve your strategic position.

Many businesses, and their leaders, are focused on problem solving ahead of innovation, however. Of course, you need a mix of both, but the key issue is where your real focus is. Using Figure 5.2, there are four quadrants for you to consider. If you were to divide all your time and focus, what share would you attach to each quadrant?

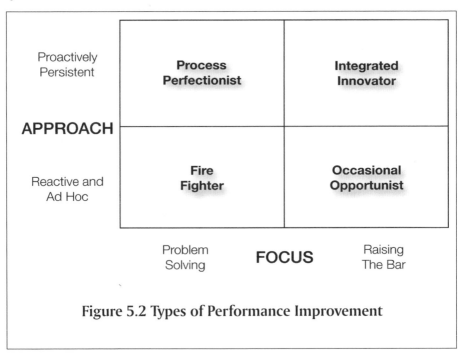

Figure 5.2 Types of Performance Improvement

In my experience, 70% or more of the attention of most chief executives is devoted to problem solving, and up to 50% of it is on 'fire fighting', resolving issues as they arise. If you wish to gain a stronger position in your market you must devote a bigger share of your time and effort to systematic innovation efforts; you must become an 'integrated innovator'.

Becoming an 'integrated innovator' means that you are continuously seeking to raise the bar. Raising the bar is more, far more, than simply setting bigger goals. In fact, when AG Lafley became CEO of Procter & Gamble, he simultaneously drove systematic innovation into the organization *and* reduced the future performance goals that he set for the business.

Here are six ways you can raise the bar and create a more innovative business.

1. **Become more future-focused.** Problem solving is based on what's happened in the past. If you're more focused on the future you are looking at how you can make Version #10 of your new product great, and not simply spending your time resolving all of the issues associated with Version #1. *How much of your time are you focused on future trends and opportunities?*

2. **Become more outward looking and customer focused.** This is more than undertaking research. It means spending real time with customers, experiencing your products and services from where they stand, and identifying their frustrations and hidden needs. *How much time do you spend each week with your customers?*

3. **Embrace prudent risk taking.** There is no growth without risk. You do not always have to bet the farm, but by accepting and working with a certain level of risk you can focus on maximising the upside from your new ideas. *What balance of risk vs. return are you prepared to take with new ventures?*

4. **Acknowledge the inevitability of failure.** Failure is the Siamese twin of innovation. The secret is to fail as fast and cheaply as possible. Using prototypes, getting your ideas out there and learning as you go are critical approaches to driving strategic advantages from innovation. *What is your attitude to the failure of early trials and prototypes?*

5. **Push accountability through the organization.** Innovation cannot happen on the top corridor. It takes place in the outer reaches of your organization. For innovation to become systemic, you need people to feel both empowered and accountable for their actions to bring new ideas to your customers. *How active are your front-line teams in suggesting and developing new ideas to grow your business?*

It is not enough, however, to decide to be more innovative. If you wish to make rapid and sustainable progress you must also align your innovation with your strategy. Innovation is not just about new product development. Most of the innovation literature focuses on the companies that excel in developing new game-changing products and services, but this is only one aspect of innovation. It is also possible to innovate around your operating system, your organizational design, your use of certain assets, and how you inspire and motivate your people. The critical factor is that to drive consistent success, the focus of your innovation should be aligned and integrated with your strategic priorities.

Strategic Focus And customer reactions	Key Capabilities	Innovation Focus
Product Leader "It costs more, but it's worth it"	• New product development • Ad-hoc project management • Managing product life cycles	• Products that set, not follow, customer demands
Cost Leader "I can't believe the value"	• Cost management • Offer and process simplification • No-frills operations	• Cost and price reduction
Convenience Leader "It's all so hassle-free"	• Operating excellence • Standardisation and systemisation • Process management	• Quicker, more reliable and more convenient operations
Service Leader "They offer such great advice and support"	• Front-line technical expertise • Operating excellence • Front-line people skills	• Helping customers every step of the way
Solutions Leader "It's exactly the solution I was after"	• Developing bespoke solutions • Building strong, effective customer relationships • Empowering front-line teams	• Customisation and personalisation

Figure 5.3 Aligning Innovation With Your Strategic Focus

Figure 5.3 sets out the focus for innovation for each of the five competitive strategies, together with the supporting capabilities required. A *Product Leader* such as Nike, for example, will be relentlessly introducing new products and technologies, managing their life cycle and, as demand declines, withdrawing and replacing that particular model. Nike's product managers will be less concerned about finding new ways to keep costs to an absolute minimum, although this will be the prime focus for the managers of a *Cost Leader* such as Aldi. Similarly, McDonalds, as a *Convenience Leader*, doesn't spend all of its time on product innovation or trying to re-invent the Big Mac. Instead, its managers focus on finding new, more efficient and reliable ways to manage its supply chain, and improve the convenience for its customers (e.g. drive-thru's, 24-hour restaurants).

As we've discussed, all companies need to be competitive on most, if not all, of the five dimensions. You must therefore spend sufficient time and effort raising the bar and driving sufficient innovation on each competitive strategy . The critical point, however, is that you should put your organization's shoulder behind your preferred strategic focus so that you can create true differentiation for your customers and higher levels of growth for your business. Some companies can, over time, establish strategic and innovation leadership on more than one dimension. Coca-Cola and Bentley, for example, are both *Product Leaders*, but have been able to innovate on more than one dimension. Bentley, the luxury carmaker, also offers its customers market-leading service support, sending engineers to your home, if necessary, to resolve any problems you may have. Coca-Cola, on the other hand, has added convenience to its brand domination. You can buy Coke virtually anywhere – high-end bars, fast-food restaurants, grocery stores, convenience stores, vending machines – enabling the company to put Coke within reach of most consumers.

These dual strategies can only be developed over time, however, and, critically, you must be famous for one of the competitive strategy dimensions before you can expect to make material progress on a second front.

From The Top: Najib Fayad

Najib Fayad is the COO of Nelson & Co Limited, the UK's largest manufacturer of natural healthcare products. The company has a turnover of over $70 million, and operations in the UK, Europe and the USA.

Nelsons is a family-owned business. The positive thing about this is that we're not tied to quarter-by-quarter results and can focus on longer-term priorities. But this only happens when our owners are fully committed and engaged with our strategic direction – and that is an emotional as much as it's an analytical exercise.

When we built our new strategy we made sure that we didn't use numbers or P&L's until we'd settled on an overall intent. Our early discussions were focused on what was happening in our markets, what the customer and consumer trends were and how well placed we were as a business to exploit some key emerging opportunities. Importantly, our conversations were not just about listing our assets, capabilities and threats but also about identifying common values and agreeing what, as a leadership team, we were passionate about.

From this work, we created what I call a 'Pre-strategy Vision' highlighting possible directions for the company, my own preferences and reasoning and then, only then, what this might mean at a very high level for our financials.

As we gained alignment and agreement on the Vision we then identified a handful of key objectives, established initial plans to take the business forward and engaged our people in what the strategy meant for them. The fact that the strategy is focused, has been developed in simple, everyday language and is not over-burdened by financial forecasts has meant that it has been easy for our people to 'get it'. Everyone in the organization understands where they fit in and what role they play in delivering our ambitions as a group.

Perhaps unsurprisingly, we have doubled in size in the past few years, but our current ambitions are even higher.

Driving New Growth: Think and Act Bigger

Becoming more aware of the need to raise the bar and innovate continuously leads almost immediately to the next question: how do you take your business to the next level of growth? The answer to that question has good news and bad news. The good news is that there are many options open to you and it's your choice to decide; the bad news is that there are many options open to you and it's your choice to decide. There are no right and wrong answers, but a few general principles can help steer you in the right direction:

- **Principle #1: Your core business often has more potential for growth than you think.** When faced with the first signs of a performance plateau many business leaders, after trying to improve the efficiency of their business, look to a diversification strategy as the best way forward. All the evidence, however, suggests that diversification is the least likely route to profitable growth. It is generally better to refocus on your core business and identify ways in which it can be re-energized, made available to new customers and more relevant to existing customers. For example, Alan Mullaly, the CEO of the motor giant, Ford, led the company's turnaround from a loss of $12.7 billion in 2006 to a profit of $6.6 billion in 2011. He did this not by buying businesses but by selling them. In the intervening years Ford sold Aston Martin, Land Rover, Jaguar and Volvo and halted the production of the Mercury brand so that he and the rest of the business could focus on the core brand, Ford.

- **Principle #2: You are likely to have organizational assets and capabilities that can help you access new, adjacent markets**. Most academic reports suggest that the best way to drive profitable new growth is a "core +" strategy. What the academics mean is that focusing on your core business while also making moves into adjacent markets will tend to drive the largest improvement in shareholder value. Over time, as your moves into adjacent markets become embedded as your core business, you can then make further moves away from your traditional business. One of my clients, Nectar, the UK's leading retail coalition loyalty program, added an insights and communications division to its business, helping retailers and their suppliers to mine the customer data created by the loyalty program to better focus their marketing, product development and merchandizing activities.

■ **Principle #3: You don't have to do it all on your own.** Over the past decade there has been an explosion in the use of partnerships, sometimes between competing companies, to help drive mutual performance improvements. Using a partner to give you access to complementary capabilities and assets you don't have helps you to fast-track your growth and also minimise the risk associated with major new investments. In addition, although most acquisitions are focused on providing scale and efficiency to core operations, many are focused on acquiring new skills or access to new markets. Tesco, for example, has combined partnerships and focused acquisitions to help it learn how to grow its businesses in South East Asia. These alliances and acquisitions have not only given Tesco access to new assets, they also helped managers better understand the shopping habits and needs of customers with very different tastes to those in Tesco's home market of the UK.

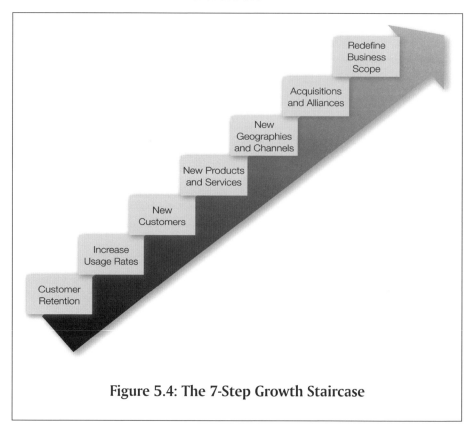

Figure 5.4: The 7-Step Growth Staircase

Using these principles, Figure 5.4 sets out a growth staircase for you to use to drive the growth of your business. There are seven steps for you to take:

1. **Improve customer retention.** Many studies have shown that it's far more efficient and profitable to improve the retention of existing customers than it is to attract new customers to fill the hole by those who no longer buy from you (although why you need a study to prove this kind of common sense point, I'm not sure). Using special offers and deals to attract new buyers is one thing, but customers will only stay with you if you can provide them with longer-term value. At the top-end of the market, Singapore Airlines creates highly loyal customers through its customer service excellence. But you don't have to offer expensive products to create loyalty. McDonalds dominates its market and retains customers by providing a mix of brand attractiveness, product quality, price and convenience that its competitors cannot match. For any company, steps to improve retention include:

   ◆ *Monitoring customer satisfaction and retention.* Do you know your customers' level of satisfaction, areas of dissatisfaction, the number and potential value of past customers who have not bought from you in the last 6 or 12 months, or where those 'lost' customers are now buying these goods and services? Without this kind of information you are unlikely to be able to manage retention effectively. Managing satisfaction and retention is just as critical as managing costs. Most organizations have cost accountants by the dozen, but I've yet to meet a satisfaction and retention accountant!

   ◆ *Enhancing the customer experience.* Using the data you collect on satisfaction, loyalty and retention, your next task is to identify where you can improve the quality of service. Following a downturn in performance, the founder of Starbucks, Howard Schultz, returned to the business in 2008. Since then the fortunes of the company have improved and a key element of that improvement has been a focus on enhancing the customer experience. Improvements in service quality and speed, store presentation, coffee quality and the offering of new, healthier options have all responded to customers' concerns and helped drive recent growth in sales and profits.

◆ *Developing customer relationships and communities.* Many retailers now use loyalty programs to create a closer relationship with their customers. These programs have the added value of providing the retailer with a better understanding of their customers' shopping habits (helping to monitor retention, as discussed above), but also the discounts, treats and special offers generated by these programs give customers an extra reason to shop with the retailer again. These approaches work in business-to-business sectors also. One of my clients, a manufacturer of products to the plumbing trade, has successfully launched an "installers' club" where it offers qualified installers of its products higher levels of training, special offers and involvement in its new product development activity. Other less formal relationships and communities can also be effective. Customer product ratings on Amazon's site have helped create a relationship between the company and its customers above and beyond previous transactional websites.

2. **Increase the usage rates of your products and services**. A common by-product of improving customer retention is that your customers also buy from you more frequently. But you can also grow usage directly. A marketing star in Procter & Gamble, for example, once had the breakthrough idea of adding the words "rinse and repeat" to the instructions on their shampoo bottles, driving up usage overnight (or, at least, first thing in the morning). The fashion industry's *raison d'être* has been the continuous creation of new seasonal collections, attracting customers to come back to their stores more frequently, and this approach has been adopted in other sectors. Swatch, for example, turned watches from a product in which consumers had one or maybe two products, to an industry where customers have a collection to choose from.

From my experience of retail loyalty programs I also know that once a shopper enjoys her well-earned reward – either in the form of discounts, using loyalty points to buy 'free' products, or spending their vouchers – they tend to become more loyal to the program and spend more with that retailer. At first glance, a retail finance director may wish to limit their customers' desire to take advantage of these rewards, but this really is a false economy once the increase in usage rates is understood.

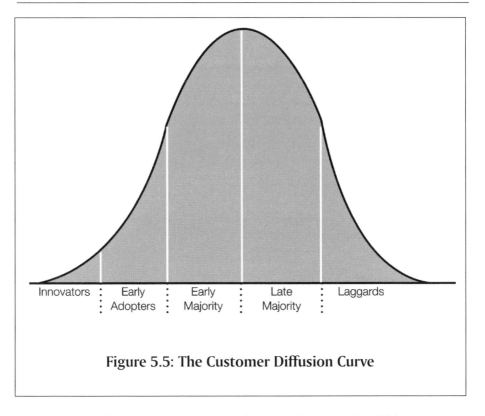

Innovators : Early : Early : Late : Laggards
: Adopters : Majority : Majority :

Figure 5.5: The Customer Diffusion Curve

3. **Attract and retain new customers**. There are three ways in which companies can attract new customers:

◆ *Convert non-users*. Many technology companies drive growth primarily by persuading non-users to buy their products. Using the customer diffusion curve, set out in Figure 5.5, you can see that the bulk of the market only buys into a new innovation once the early adopters are satisfied that it is a success. Managing and influencing that buy-in process is critical to their success. At a consumer level, for example, Sony's Walkman, Apple's iPod and the Nintendo Wii have been able to reach the middle and right hand sections of the chart, whereas both Betamax and MiniDiscs failed to get past the early adopter stage. The key to successful conversion is to have highly satisfied early adopters who sing the praises of your product or service, influencing the next level of customers to try you out.

◆ *Find new uses and customer segments*. The pharmaceutical industry has a history of re-assigning drugs for new treatments. Sometimes the pharmaceutical company will produce lower-strength treatments for less severe conditions. Glaxo, for instance, first produced Zantac as a prescription-only medicine to treat peptic ulcers, but the company has also developed lower-strength products to aid the treatment of heartburn. In other instances, the side-effects of the product became the core proposition. Viagra, for example, was originally developed as a potential treatment for angina. It was only once the side-effects became apparent that Pfizer redirected its development to combat erectile dysfunction!

But it is not only pharmacos that find new uses and segments for their products. Land Rover has, over time, extended its product line of four-wheel drive vehicles from simply being the farmers' transport of choice and into lifestyle cars for modern families, both in the city and the country. Mobile phone companies have also segmented their customers and provide very different handsets and services for teenagers than they do for business customers. The question you must ask yourself is what customer segments could you serve that you are currently missing, and how could you refocus your existing proposition to make it attractive to these new groups.

◆ *Take share from competitors.* In the past taking share meant two things: spending more on advertising and offering lower prices. The proliferation of media channels and of new products has meant that neither of these steps are, on their own, likely to generate success. Instead, winning business from competitors is now the result of the actions you take on the first three steps on the growth staircase. Managing satisfaction and retention, enhancing the customer experience, creating communities and stronger customer relationships, building loyalty, proactively managing the customer diffusion curve and finding new uses that appeal to specific customer segments are the ways in which, over time, recommendations and word-of-mouth will attract customers away from their current providers.

4. **Offer new products and services**. The extension of your current offerings into new lines is the fourth step of the growth staircase. There are offensive and defensive reasons for developing new products and services. Offensively, it can generate significant new revenues for

your business and maintain or grow the gap between the value of your customer proposition and those of your competitors. But defensively, you have no choice. The explosion of new product development, the pace of technological advancements and the relentless rise in global competition means that if you don't continue to innovate your products and services will simply become obsolete. There are three valuable forms of product and service expansion:

◆ *Dramatically improving your current products.* Gillette, for example, has created new ranges of razors that continue to keep it ahead of its competition. Starting with the *Gillette Sensor* in 1990, the company then introduced *Sensor Excel* in 1995, the *Mach3* in 1998 (including the battery-driven *M3 Power*), the *Fusion* range in 2006, and the *Fusion ProGlide* in 2010. At each stage the performance improvement offered by the new range not only outclassed the competition, but made Gillette's existing ranges redundant. Gillette's management knew that it was better that they cannibalized their own sales than let one of their competitors do it for them.

◆ *Extending existing ranges.* As Gillette's razor technology improved it was able to develop a new range, Venus, designed specifically for women. Not only did this generate new revenues for the business, but improved the confidence of men across the world that their razor would be as sharp when they picked it up as it was when they last used it! Other companies add different flavours, product-type or pack sizes to extend their ranges. One of my clients, Nelsons Natural Healthcare, which manufactures and markets homeopathic treatments, has, for example, added to the ways in which customers can use their Rescue Remedy range products by introducing sprays, pastilles and even chewing gum products.

◆ *Moving into new, adjacent markets.* The bigger move from the development of new products and services is the decision to enter entirely new markets. Some companies are able to make major leaps, but expansion into adjacent markets is more likely to lead to profitable growth. Using and exploiting existing capabilities and assets, as well as acquiring some new ones, helps to create new growth at an acceptable level of risk. The critical issue is to ensure that your existing capabilities and assets are relevant to the new market you are entering. Starbucks, for instance, is succeeding with the development of its own instant coffee brands to use at home, but failed dismally with its attempts at producing and marketing CD's, which was a step too far for the business.

5. **Enter new geographies and channels**. Taking your business to new customers can mean entering new channels and geographies. The prize from geographical expansion can be huge, as it allows you to replicate your existing formula for success. Up until its merger with Caremark, CVS, the US drug store chain, for example, had driven its growth primarily on the basis of adding new stores in new states across the USA. The company avoided international expansion as the growth provided by its domestic market more than met shareholders' growth expectations. Channel expansion also offers major profit growth opportunities. Dell originally only sold its products directly, but you can now buy Dell PC's in retail outlets. Similarly, a key element of Apple's recent success has been the growth of its own store chain, enabling the company to avoid sharing margins with other retailers and giving it greater control over customers' shopping experience.

Expansion – whether geographical or into new channels – will only succeed, however, if you have capabilities that provide you with manifest competitive advantages. Many companies are seeking to expand into the high-growth markets of China, India and Brazil, but they will only succeed if they can offer real customer value at an acceptable cost of delivery. Vodafone, the European mobile phone operator, pulled out of its Chinese venture in order to maintain its development focus on its core European and African markets. The market may have been large, but Vodafone simply could not find a winning competitive position.

6. **Invest in partnerships and acquisitions**. Where you do not have the necessary assets or capabilities to deliver your growth ambitions, and you are unlikely to be able to develop them organically, acquisitions and alliances provide a fast-track route to growth. Studies have shown that in many industries, acquisitions can deliver 50% or more of successful companies' profit growth. BAE Systems, the UK-based defense manufacturer, has driven significant growth through the acquisition of companies to drive greater scale and efficiency in existing

markets, as well as helping it develop market-leading positions in adjacent markets. For example, the company developed its "land" business (which provides vehicles, equipment and armaments for land armies) as a further set of solutions for its existing customers – major governments across the world. This growth initiative was driven by the company's acquisition of three existing land defense businesses – Alvis, United Defense and Armor Holdings. BAE System's management then integrated these disparate companies into a single commercial division with the scale and reach to operate on the global stage.

Partnerships are a viable and increasingly popular alternative to acquisition. Partnerships provide access to new customers and capabilities, but at a lower cost. These arrangements allow all the parties involved to share risk, albeit at lower levels of return. The former Procter & Gamble CEO, AG Lafley, turned the consumer giant's traditional in-house development on its head when he set a target that 50% of new product ideas should be sourced from outside the company in order to accelerate the company's level of innovation and growth. As with acquisitions, partnerships require the development of specific management capabilities, and these are best developed in smaller, less risky initiatives before being applied to bigger deals.

7. **Redefine your business scope**. The ultimate business growth initiative is the wholesale redefinition of your business. When Steve Jobs returned to Apple in 1997 he changed the scope of the business from being a developer of personal computers into the creator of personal electronic devices. The words of this change may seem simple, but the impact has been profound. The company's traditional product, the Mac, now accounts for just a quarter of total sales. The company's growth has been turbo-charged by the development of the iPhone, iPod and related products, services and software. If Apple had continued to see itself as a personal computer business, as companies such as Compaq did, it would never have made these major strategic moves or delivered a fraction of the growth it has achieved.

Growth, Innovation and Good Failure vs. Bad Failure

The common theme across these seven ways to drive new growth is the need to innovate. Simply doing more of the same is unlikely to lead to sustainable success.

The Darwinian rules of business mean you must be constantly looking to adapt and evolve in order to remain relevant to the fast-changing world. As you progress up the growth staircase, the risks associated with failure increase, increasing the need for effective risk management. This doesn't mean that you avoid risk – prudent risk-taking is at the heart of commercial success – but that you develop preventative and contingent plans for any major possible downsides.

The effective management of failure within your growth strategy is clearly illustrated by looking at how a couple of major UK retailers – Marks & Spencer and Tesco – managed major new growth initiatives in the late 1990s and early 2000s. These examples demonstrate the difference between 'good failure' and 'bad failure' within an innovation process.

Marks & Spencer, better known as M&S, is a leading UK retailer offering food, fashion and household goods to relatively affluent, middle-class families. In 1997 it became the first British retailer to deliver £1 billion profits, but by the early 2000s it was struggling to compete with lower-priced rivals in all of its key categories. Better quality grocery competition was hitting food sales, specialist fashion retailers, including Next, The Gap and H&M, were making the M&S offer appear old-fashioned, and IKEA's low-price furniture stores were attracting younger, more value-conscious shoppers. By 2001, its profit performance had plummeted to £145 million.

The executive team at M&S battled hard to combat these pressures, launching new fashion brands and food lines, closing its struggling international business, and launching a food-only format, *M&S Simply Food*. While these steps helped to improve profits back to over £500 million, they were still nowhere near its previous highs.

The new CEO, Roger Holmes, had brought in Vittorio Radice, the former CEO of Selfridges, one of London's iconic department stores, to revamp the chain's look and feel. In 2003 Holmes and Radice announced that the company was launching a new concept, the *M&S Lifestore*. The *Lifestore* format was announced with much hype and fanfare, and was focused on homewares only – furniture, lighting, dining, kitchen and household accessories. Unlike the core store chain, the *Lifestore* was a radically new shopping experience. Instead of a store laid out along traditional departmental lines, it featured themed spaces that included a complete house designed by the minimalist designer John Pawson.

The first store was built in Gateshead and the company reportedly invested £60 million behind Mr Radice's vision, which included a dramatic restructuring of the range to more chic styles, an increase in the number of lines to over 12,000 items, and the investment in the Gateshead store. Unsurprisingly, however, the concept failed. It simply didn't fit with the needs and desires of M&S's core customers and it didn't address the pricing issue that had been raised by IKEA. Under pressure from shareholders and facing a hostile takeover bid, the board sacked Mr Holmes and Mr Radice, bringing in Sir Stuart Rose to lead the troubled retailer back to more sustainable growth, which included the immediate closure of the failing experimental store.

M&S's *Lifestore* concept was a bad failure: bad for Holmes and Radice, of course, but also bad for investors, who saw the share price of the business fall, bad for customers, who became confused about the values and proposition of the retailer, and also bad for the organization, which saw its reputation and its self-confidence depleted.

But not all failures are bad. On the contrary, many failures are good, and are simply part of the learning that is necessary to succeed. One example of good failure is the development of Tesco's *Express* store format. Tesco is one of the world's largest grocers and, in the UK, accounts for £1 in every £6 spent in the nation's shops. During the 1990s the company, under the leadership of Terry Leahy, created a new growth strategy, one leg of which was the development of distinctive store formats. As part of this format development program the company identified the convenience channel as an opportunity for growth. Yet, despite its name *Tesco Express* was anything but. There was no overnight success for the model. In fact it took over 6 years for the company to get over 20 stores off the ground. Express by name? Yes. Overnight success? Hardly.

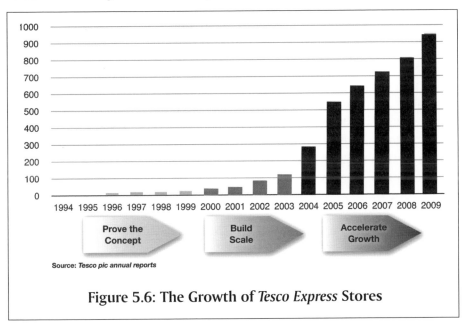

Source: Tesco plc annual reports

Figure 5.6: The Growth of *Tesco Express* Stores

Tesco's convenience concept was developed in 1993 and the first store was on the ground the following year. However, as demonstrated in Figure 5.6, even five years later there were little more than a dozen stores. In fact you can detect three key periods of development:

- **1994-1999 – Prove The Concept.** By 1999 there were 17 stores, and the Annual Report quietly noted that *Tesco Express* was becoming a "promising format". Behind the scenes, the format development team were busy developing and testing many different variants of the store, so that a model that was appealing to customers, operationally effective and financially attractive could be rolled out. The end result of this concept development period was the announcement in 1999 of a joint venture with Esso, where *Tesco Express* stores would be introduced to more than 100 Esso gas stations.

- **1999-2003 – Build Scale.** The deal with Esso created new store opportunities for Tesco. The 100 Esso stores that were added over the next four years enabled the *Tesco Express* format to reach a level of scale, delivering sales of up to $500 million. The format was ready for its next stage of development.

- **2003 onwards – Accelerate Growth.** Having built a sustainable business, Tesco then set about accelerating the chain's growth and becoming the UK's convenience store market leader. Critical to this stage was Tesco's acquisition of the T&S Convenience stores chain, which they quickly rebranded to *Tesco Express*. Further deals and store openings followed this acquisition and by 2011 the company had approximately 1,000 *Tesco Express* stores, delivering in the region of $5 billion in annual sales.

The critical point in this story, however, is how the ultimate success of *Tesco Express* is built on the tests, trials and, lets face it, the failures of the early years of the program. Without these failures, the success of the format would not have happened. Figure 5.7 contrasts the approach of the Tesco team to the development of their Express format with that of the M&S executives and the development of their *Lifestore* concept.

	Tesco Express	M&S Lifestore
	Build off a strong core business	Build off a weak core business
	Just one of the growth opportunities across a portfolio of programs	Seen as the 'silver bullet' solution to the company's problems
	Only roll out the format once the customer, operating and economic models all work	Plan the roll-out of the concept across the chain before the model has been tested and developed
	Continue commitment to the program in the face of early setbacks	Shut down the program when initial results are not favourable
	Manage external expectations downwards in the early stages	Build up external expectations even before the first centre is built
	Use partners, joint ventures and acquisitions to accelerate growth	Seek to deliver the whole solution internally and organically

Figure 5.7: Developing a new growth opportunity –
Tesco Express vs. M&S *Lifestore*

Key Points

- Many companies fail, not because they are bad at what they do, but because they are great at what they do. Beware of the perils of success!
- Sustainable, ongoing growth demands that you continue to raise the bar and use your existing success as a springboard for further growth
- Your innovation activities should follow your strategic focus
- There are seven steps on the growth staircase, but it starts with retaining your existing customers
- Failure is an inevitable aspect of innovation and growth – the goal should not be to avoid failure, but to fail as quickly and cheaply as possible
- Creating a new business concept follows three phases: proving the concept; building scale; and accelerating growth

Chapter 6

BRINGING YOUR HIGH-LEVEL STRATEGY DOWN TO EARTH

Preparing For Ground-Level Success

Don't Get Lost In Translation

High-level strategy is as useful to most workers in an organization as a high-flying airliner is to people in a bus queue. The bus passengers may briefly look up and notice the plane and its vapor trail, but, even if it is traveling in the same direction, it cannot possibly help them reach their destination. Similarly, unless you can bring your strategy down-to-earth it will have no discernible effect on your organization's performance, or, worse, it will create confusion, paralysis and decline.

It is often said that a strategy doesn't fail in its formulation but in its implementation. I don't agree. I believe that in many cases strategy simply falls through the gap between formulation and implementation: it fails in its *translation*. Many leadership teams, in their excitement and enthusiasm to turn their strategy into reality, fail to take the necessary steps to ensure that the strategy is sufficiently grounded and that the organization is able and geared up to deliver it.

A $500 million consumer services business I worked with had invested heavily in developing a compelling new strategy and direction. The executive team was excited about the new opportunities that were being uncovered and had set ambitious and demanding growth targets, and changed the performance measures accordingly. The CEO and his senior executives had also spent time with front-line service managers communicating the vision and the high-level strategy for achieving it. However, over the following months the CEO became increasingly frustrated that the organization was failing to make sufficient progress towards the new goals and targets.

As we investigated we quickly discovered that there were three barriers preventing the organization from delivering the new strategic agenda:

1. **Individual accountabilities had not been re-set.** Managers had the new KPIs, but their own performance objectives had not changed. Individual success criteria did not reflect the new organizational success criteria, and there was general confusion about what was expected.

2. **Talent had not been re-deployed.** The new agenda demanded that the people across the business work differently, with a far greater focus on providing an outstanding customer experience. The roles, however, were exactly the same as the previous strategy. The best people were still in their previous positions and there were no clear champions for the new, ambitious growth agenda.

3. **Resources had not been re-allocated.** Underpinning these failures was the fact that resources had not been proactively reallocated away from the old activities and projects and into the new priorities. In essence, the projects that were driving the old strategy were simply re-packaged under the new one, and none had been dropped or fundamentally re-scoped.

The result of these failures was that the organization made little progress. The situation was like that of a novice rider trying to get a stubborn horse to move. There was a lot of shouting about what the company wanted to do coming from the saddle, but the executive team were unable to shift their collective weight and provide the required kick-start to get the organization moving in the right direction. They failed to translate their high-level intentions into focused action on the ground. They were lost in translation.

You cannot leave your strategy at 50,000 feet. The success of your team or business is based on your ability to bring it down-to-earth so that your people can implement it and deliver 'ground-breaking' results. Figure 6.1 highlights the importance of connecting the high-level strategy at 50,000 feet into operational success on the ground. The 50,000 feet strategic vision is all about identifying your key performance goals, the scope of your business, how you will compete and win in your chosen markets, and what capabilities you want your organization to develop. On the ground, selecting appropriate initiatives and managing projects, programmes and overall performance effectively drives operational success.

Between these two extremes lie the tasks of translating the strategic vision and of creating the conditions for your strategy to be delivered by managers and teams across the organization. This is a leadership, not a management task. It is focused on helping your people understand the group's goals and priorities, providing them with the tools and know-how to make it happen, and ensuring that their rewards – both material and emotional – are aligned with your organizations' agreed objectives.

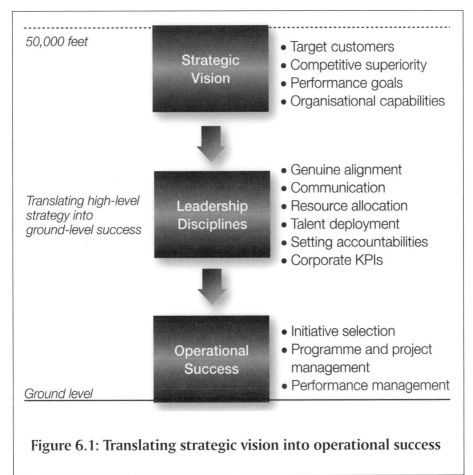

Figure 6.1: Translating strategic vision into operational success

As CEO, this is perhaps your most important role and one that you must be seen to lead. People believe what they see and experience, not what they read or hear. Translating your strategic vision therefore involves a mix of decision-making, persuasion and acting as an exemplar. Too often, however, it is a role that is overlooked and many CEOs can become trapped either at 50,000 feet, developing and refining their vision and values, or, more commonly, at ground level, where all their effort is focused on managing the day-to-day operational performance of the business. Success requires focus, discipline and repetition so that the behaviours become habits rather than one-off actions.

As set out in Figure 6.1 the translation process involves six leadership disciplines:

1. **Creating genuine alignment.** When I was younger I used to ski on the Scottish Cairngorms. Each morning I would check the weather, knowing that the slightest hint of a breeze down in the glen would mean that a gale would be blowing on the exposed mountains. Executive alignment is very similar to the weather conditions in the Cairngorms. Tiny differences of opinion in the boardroom can become huge divisions across the organization, rapidly reducing your chances of successful implementation. A lack of executive alignment can bring your organization to a standstill. And the resistance to your new direction does not have to be an active revolution; passive resistance, where executives don't argue against the strategy, but just fail to do anything to implement it, is equally dangerous.

   Alignment is best developed through genuine involvement. I know a CEO who joined a new company where the previous CEO was highly autocratic, and where even senior executives were merely given tasks to implement. In his first six months, the CEO focused on involving his new team in creating a shared strategic direction. The result was an improvement in the quality of the strategy, but more importantly a step change in the level of engagement and belief in the resulting agenda across the leadership team. For the first time, the executives had the opportunity to debate the company's big issues, assess alternative ways forward and agree the trade-offs required to improve the company's performance.

2. **Relentless communication.** The strategic intent should form the basis of all communication across the organization. Communication isn't so much about the big conventions and set-piece events, it's about the corridor conversations and one-to-one meetings you have whether it's in your office or on the front-line. More importantly, it's not even driven

by what you say, but by what people across the business say about you. From the decisions you make, the actions and programs you set in train, and the way you engage others in meetings and conversations, what would your team (and your team's teams) say were your strategic priorities? If the answer is not the same as the 'official' written strategy statement you may as well ignore the 'official' version; everyone else will be.

3. **Resource allocation.** Resources should be allocated on their ability to deliver the agreed strategy, and not simply reflect historic trends and decisions. The allocation of your scarce resources is the crunch time for your strategy; it's where the rubber hits the road, where people will determine whether or not you're walking the talk and see if you mean business (further clichés available on request!). Seriously, your strategy is only as effective as your willingness and ability to invest the necessary resources – financial, people or key assets – to help deliver the results you're after.

4. **Talent deployment and development.** Your best and most able people should be leading the delivery of your key strategic priorities. Not only does this increase your chances of success, but it also sends a signal to the organization about what you consider important. I have noticed that in some companies middle and aspiring managers are reticent about becoming involved in strategic initiatives. They feel more comfortable, and better able to manage and develop their careers, staying in their line roles, rather than taking on something that may be new and unproven. My perspective of the companies where this happens is that the organizational culture does not reward risk-taking well, and one failure can end the career for a high-potential manager. If you want to attract your best people into these critical roles, you must give them the best chance to succeed, but you should also demonstrably promote successful leaders out of these strategic roles. That way, your strategic initiatives will be seen as a gateway to success, and not the organization's main exit.

5. **Setting accountabilities.** Individual performance, and the collective performance of the top team, should be directly based on implementing the strategy. This requires breaking down your strategic objectives and programs into lower-level objectives that can be owned

and delivered by managers across the business. At one of my clients, the CEO worked with his executive colleagues to break down the company's biggest priorities into specific targets and objectives. For each objective, the executive team identified the line manager best placed to deliver it, with each executive director owning the objectives most relevant to themselves. At each performance review meeting – individual and team sessions – the CEO now uses this summary of objectives and accountabilities (he calls it his *Leadership Agenda*) to hold his management team to account. By embedding accountabilities, the CEO has ensured that the strategy is part of the company's everyday activities, and not something that happens when the 'day job' has been completed.

6, **Agreeing corporate KPIs.** Your KPIs should mirror your strategy, as should your associated rewards and bonuses. Have you, for example, set a high-level strategy around innovative new growth, and yet remain fixated on monthly margins and costs? If so, don't be surprised that your managers pay less attention to innovation and more to the current year's financials. If you are serious about your strategy you will find ways to track its delivery effectively. Focusing your reporting around KPIs, and not just project plans, also ensures that people remain focused on delivering results and not just managing tasks. At one of my clients, for instance, strategic projects were historically managed through action plans. By augmenting this approach with a small set of KPIs for each of the key programs, managers quickly took ownership for their programs' results and also became more demanding of their colleagues in providing support and resources for these initiatives that, in the past, were implemented but not fully embedded in the way the company did business.

The Strategy Routemap: Aligning Short-Term Demands With Longer-Term Objectives

I once read a survey that suggested that more than half of all Chief Finance Officers would cut a project with a positive net present value in order to hit short-term profit targets. In other words, these CFOs would forsake future profits to meet immediate aims. There is, of course, a certain level of logic to this behavior, but a persistently short-term focus is damaging for company performance. A recent study showed that the returns to shareholders of companies that delivered short-term and long-term results were nearly 50% greater than those solely focused on the short-term.

Although many companies aspire to balancing short-term results and long-term growth, external pressures and internal processes mean that strategy development activities quickly turn into a budget-setting exercise. And if that happens it is the urgent, short-term demands that win every time.

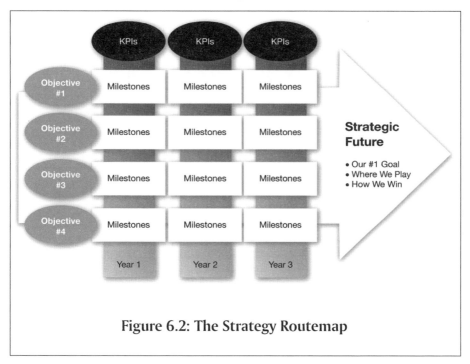

Figure 6.2: The Strategy Routemap

So what can you do to manage the conflicts between your immediate issues and your longer-term goals? One tool that has proven popular with my clients is *The Strategy Routemap* (see Figure 6.2). The framework acts as a bridge between your strategy and goals, as set out in your *Strategy Arrow* that we discussed in Chapter 3, to your operating plans and budgets, which we shall cover in Chapter 7. Here are the steps you should take to create a routemap that will drive decisions and actions in line with your strategy:

1. Start by clarifying and summarizing the arrowhead of your strategy; your #1 goal, where you will play and how you will win.

2. For each of your handful of agreed strategic objectives identify the major achievements and milestones you need to accomplish over

the next few years in order to hit your goal and deliver your strategy. Summarize these milestones, by year, on the chart.

3. For your #1 goal, and other key performance measures, establish top-down targets by year.

4. Establish accountabilities for delivery for each of your objectives and critical milestones, naming a specific manager or executive to lead each one.

5. Once you have developed and agreed your strategy routemap, you can then align your bottom-up plans and actions to your top-down objectives and milestones. If you find that you are running, or are planning to launch, projects that fall outside your strategic ambitions you should drop them from your agenda.

6. Where you don't have any projects or plans against a particular strategic objective or milestone, develop alternative solutions and select those with the best overall return.

7. For each of your projects ensure that your named leaders develop initial plans to take them forward. Review overall forecast levels of sales and profit improvement against your key performance measures. Where you fail to meet your top-down targets, request that your leaders develop alternative plans for at least some of your projects, ensuring that you allocate resources only when you are confident that you can meet your performance standards.

8. Remember that the work to achieve your longer-term milestones may need to begin immediately. It is therefore worth splitting your projects into two types: implementation projects, where you have identified the solution and are driving current year performance; and development projects, where you are still determining the solutions required to drive future years' performance. As you review your agenda of initiatives, ensure that you have an appropriate balance between implementation and development projects.

The benefits of this approach are threefold. First, you start with your strategy and major objectives and work back from there. You are not simply seeking to identify ways to improve performance; you are looking for actions that will enhance your results *and* deliver your strategic aims. It isn't always easy to drop profitable initiatives that do not contribute to advancing your strategy, but if you fail to do this you will simply create confusion across the organization and reduce the speed and effectiveness of implementation.

Second, it pushes the accountability for the more detailed planning of projects down to the front line. You can set the pace of delivery by articulating the milestones to be met and the organization's overall performance standards, but your teams are better placed to determine what needs to be done to make these goals a reality. The critical step is to follow-up. Review the plans that your teams develop and test for speed and efficiency and ensure that, where necessary, there are cross-functional teams being established to run the projects.

Third, it helps you to focus on the journey as well as the destination. Many companies develop in-depth future strategic positions. It is less common for the equivalent effort to be put into finding the best route to delivering the strategy. It is vital to spend the time developing a suitable plan that delivers short-term performance as part of a longer-term growth campaign. Delivering short-term results is difficult for many companies, never mind spending time and effort to build longer-term growth. Yet successful companies find ways to focus on both dimensions. These practical, proven steps are ways in which they establish this dual focus.

From The Top: Hugo Reissner

Hugo Reissner is a business model development consultant and is the former CEO of CBR Fashion Holdings, a pan-European $750 million fashion brands business based in Germany

My biggest strategy management lesson is to focus as much on the "how" as on the "what". It is very easy to create a new idea for growth but I have experienced – too many times for comfort – that, if you just give the idea to your operating teams to deliver, other more urgent issues will quickly overwhelm it. As a result the new initiative fails to gain traction and fails to deliver the benefits that were targeted.

By training I am an architect. Between an architect and the craftsmen who will build the final structure that the architect designs is the building contractor. The building contractor –

'Baumeister' in German – has a pivotal role to play. In particular, he works out the best way to realise the architect's vision on the ground. This means that while he has to understand and appreciate the architect's vision and concept, he must also be able to relate to and communicate with the specialists who will actually build the structure.

It is similar with strategy. There is a key role for someone to work with the agreed ideas and work out how they can be best delivered. This is best done as a business model that describes how the envisioned pieces of a business fit together. In the business model the key questions that must be answered include:

- *Who is our customer? How do we make money and how can we deliver value to customers at an appropriate cost?*

- *What are the key stages of development for this initiative, what will it do to our current business model and how will our approach and model change at each stage?*

- *Who is best placed to deliver this initiative? Is it a specialist team or is it best delivered through the line? If the operating teams are the best owners for the initiative, what extra support and tools do they need to achieve success?*

The answers to these questions can best be delivered by a 'strategy contractor', which is a critical position to employ, externally or internally, by any company that is seeking to drive new growth.

The Secret To Effective Resource Allocation

Developing the plans that will deliver your *Strategy Routemap* requires you to allocate resources across projects and programs. But how do you achieve this on a fair and consistent basis? In my experience, few companies recognize the power of investing in strategies rather than initiatives. Most senior executives I know demand detailed discounted cash flow statements for all proposed projects. These projections must show significant payback before the initiative is considered for investment.

So what's the problem with this approach? Why is a focus on detailed initiative appraisals unhelpful? There are two major problems:

1. There is no explicit link to strategy. An initiative may make money in itself, but it can also divert focus and resources away from the company's core strategy.

2. They are open to "creative" management assumptions. Managers can tweak assumptions to create acceptable financial proposals even for dubious initiatives. For some managers this has become an art form!

A better way is to focus investment decisions on your overall strategy. It is far more difficult for managers to manipulate the financial forecasts of an overarching business strategy than it is to influence the projections of individual initiatives.

More importantly, focusing investment decisions at a strategic level requires you to make clear and consistent choices. Strategy is, at heart, about creating a system to support and deliver a distinctive proposition. In other words it is not the individual elements or initiatives that create value, but the combination of those elements working together that determines your company's success.

This point was brought home to me a few years ago by Walgreens, America's leading drugstore chain. I asked their senior managers how they could possibly get a decent payback on their drive-thru pharmacies (*"Don't they lead to lost in-store impulse sales?"*) and their 24-hour opening policy (*"How can you possibly get enough business to justify a pharmacist at 3am?"*). Their reply was revealing. The senior manager simply said, *"I don't know whether these initiatives make money in themselves, but they were both essential to our goal of being the most convenient drugstore in the US."*

By focusing resource allocation decisions on the overall strategy the initiatives became essential elements of Walgreen's agenda, whatever their economics may have looked like in isolation. Just as importantly Walgreen's management was willing to offset investment in these elements by reducing investment elsewhere - for example, low-cost store fit-outs, and lower in-store staff service levels. Management made clear choices have about where and how to invest in the customer experience and their competitive differentiation within an overall financial model.

So how do you control investment in initiatives without demanding detailed discounted cash flow forecasts? First you need to estimate the overall resource levels required to deliver the strategy over the next few years. Then, you ask three key questions for any proposed initiative:

- **Is the initiative critical to your strategy?** The key word here is 'critical'. If the initiative is only tangentially aligned with your strategic aims it is better to reject it up-front. If it has a moderate strategic fit, discuss what needs to change for it to be strongly aligned with your direction and goals. Only move onto the second question when you have ensured that its fit with your strategy is strong. Too many company agendas are littered with projects that make only a marginal contribution to either performance or strategic advancement.

- **Is this the most efficient way to fund this initiative?** Asking the project team what alternative financial models they have considered is an effective way of ensuring that you do not over-invest in the initiative. We have discussed elsewhere the importance of creating rapid-leaning, low-cost prototypes, and you should expect that your team have either already developed prototypes to help them understand the most efficient route forward, or that this is step one on their plan.

- **Can you afford the investment?** If you are filtering your projects based on their strategic fit effectively, it is amazing how much of your investment funds suddenly become available. Where the investment is still too large for your financial constraints, you should re-visit the need to look at options around different ways of funding the initiative. Otherwise, you have three broad options:

  - *Adjust the scope of the initiative until it becomes affordable.* For instance, one of my clients scaled down the pace at which it rolled out its new stores program to better balance its level of growth with the cash required to fund the company's expansion.

  - *Defer the project until a future date when you are more likely to have the necessary resources available.* Of course, the risk is that you never have the extra funds available, and the initiative never happens. That said, it might be better to wait until you can deliver the project effectively, than start immediately without having the capability to fully deliver the agreed benefits.

  - *Drop the initiative altogether.* The project may be strategically beneficial, but if you can't find a way to make it affordable you are likely to be better off focusing your efforts elsewhere. For example, I know of a retail chain that had many stores that were too large for its customer offer. Managers looked at ways to reduce the size of their stores, and even to churn the portfolio, moving from their existing locations into smaller units. However, they kept coming to the same conclusion: the investment required was simply too much to make the change worthwhile. In the end, the company dropped the project, and focused instead in creating partnerships with other retailers to better use the space.

Answering these three questions will help you determine the best way forward for your business and not just default to allocating resources to the individual initiatives with the highest cash flow projections. Making investment decisions solely at the level of detailed initiatives can hinder the longer-term performance of your business. By focusing, instead, on the value and investment of your overall strategy you will make the choices and trade-offs necessary for ultimate success.

Keep The Focus On Your Few, Big Priorities

There is a Japanese saying that translates, 'you can't chase two hares'. If a top-class hunting dog chases after a hare it has a 10% chance of catching it. But if the dog hedges its bets and tries to chase two at once, its success rate is reduced to nil. The dog quickly learns that 10% is the way to go!

It's tempting to keep our options open and pursue several different avenues. But for each avenue pursued, energy and pace is dissipated. Pushing hard on a few fronts, not pushing a little on many fronts, is the key to making substantial and rapid strategic progress.

For instance, I once helped a client develop new growth options for his business, and identified six high-potential opportunities. At the start of the decision meeting my client said, *"There's only one of these opportunities I want to pursue. It's much bigger than the other opportunities, it fits best with who we are, and we know how to pull it off. We need to focus on this one so that we can really get going."* The energy of the meeting immediately increased, plans were quickly developed and the next steps actions were immediate. As a result, the business is currently driving material sales and profit growth through this opportunity.

I know of many organizations where the executive do the work to identify a handful of strategic objectives, but then simply reallocate all the existing projects, and more, to these objectives, irrespective of whether the fit is real or imagined. In other cases, a focused agenda is set up initially, but over time becomes bloated with new, often unnecessary initiatives. Another way to get round the need to focus on a few projects is to merge some projects together. That way you can be seen to be prioritizing and still try to do everything you were trying to do before.

But the simple truth is this: complexity is the enemy of pace. And simultaneously pursuing too many priorities creates complexity. In order to succeed, people want to understand what's important and what you're not going to do, and less really is more. Prioritising effectively is not easy, and requires that you overcome these five barriers.

Barrier #1: A lack of strategic clarity. Last year a CEO told me that his executive team had identified 20 strategic priorities. Unfortunately he was unable to name more than half of them. If company leaders can't remember the strategic priorities they have decided upon, what chance do the rest of the organization have of understanding what's important, let alone of being able to deliver the agenda?

Barrier #2: A fear of missing out. If you don't know which port you're heading for, you'll always feel that you're missing the boat. You will miss out on some opportunities: get used to it. The important thing is to be making progress on the opportunities most important to your customers and your business.

Barrier #3: Corporate ego exceeding organizational capability. An honest, objective view of your organization's capacity and capability for change is critical to the successful delivery of any strategy. Even the largest businesses have a track record of over-estimating their ability to do more than a few things well. Look at the mega-mergers of AOL-Time Warner, Vodafone-Mannesmann and Daimler-Chrysler: in all these cases, management bit off much more than they could chew.

Barrier #4: Misguided risk management. When you are trying something new it is tempting to be prudent and give the initiative a low performance improvement target. The problem with this approach is that you then need to take on more initiatives in order to hit your overall targets. Figure 6.3 sets out a downward performance cycle that affects many organizations. Have you seen this cycle in your business?

- An executive team raises the bar and sets stretching goals;
- It then identifies the big initiatives that will – hopefully - deliver the organization's ambitions;
- Quickly, however, doubt creeps in and there is insufficient belief that these 'big rocks' will be able to meet the organization's stretching targets;
- More smaller initiatives are added to the agenda to give the executive team more confidence that the new performance targets will be achieved;

- But there is now too much on the organization's plate, and the desired performance fails to materialise;
- New stretching goals are set to bridge the gap, and new initiatives are agreed.

And so the cycle continues. The performance shortfall leads to further stretch goals and even more initiatives in the hope that something will work and get the company out of the hole it has dug for itself.

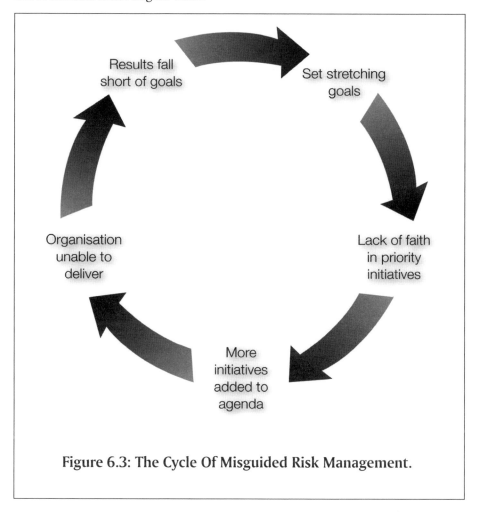

Results fall
short of goals

Set stretching
goals

Lack of faith
in priority
initiatives

More
initiatives
added to
agenda

Organisation
unable to
deliver

Figure 6.3: The Cycle Of Misguided Risk Management.

So where is the best place to break the cycle? As always it is the point that will have the biggest impact, and in this case it is the establishment of the major priorities. Executives need to critically test that these few objectives will be able to meet their performance targets. If they don't believe that achieving these objectives will be sufficient they need different, not more priorities. But if they do believe that the 'big rocks' are big enough they shouldn't respond to initial performance shortfalls by adding new projects that will simply divert management attention. They should continue to focus on their priorities and find new ways to achieve the objectives they have originally agreed.

Barrier #5: An inability to close failing projects. Many companies become clogged-up with failing projects that haven't been killed. This is precisely the wrong attitude. Innovation is built on the learning that comes from failure. Most ideas will fail, so the trick is to fail quickly and cheaply. You should be constantly weeding your 'garden' of projects to give your highest potential initiatives the opportunity to blossom and bloom.

Relentless Communication – Your Role As Chief Storyteller

I almost didn't include this topic in the book, – it all seems so obvious to write that you must communicate the strategy effectively. Yet, despite all the previous books and articles that have been written on communication, CEOs and senior executives spend too little time articulating the strategy across the organization. Effective communication of your strategy is not really a matter of reports or annual company conferences; it takes place in the thousands of smaller meetings, conversations and discussions that you have each year. Each of these sessions is an opportunity to move your strategy forwards and should not be missed.

Some CEOs, of course, are great at this. When I worked at Boots the Chemists, Richard Baker was brilliant at repeating the same message in all his communications – board meetings, newsletters, store visits, individual conversations. Richard never knowingly missed an opportunity to articulate his strategic priorities and why they were important, and, unsurprisingly, the organization quickly 'got' what the strategy was about and started to make it a reality.

Here are eight ways that you can improve your ability to communicate your company's strategy:

1. **"Keep it simple, stupid"**. If a message is to be remembered it must be simple. That's why it's so important to focus on your few, big priorities, and not try and list everything. In Bill Clinton's first presidential campaign, the internal reminder about the message was a sign that read, "It's the economy, stupid!" What's the simple focus you want to give your organization?

2. **Have your 3-5 strategic priorities to refer to in** every **discussion.** This was the cornerstone of Richard Baker's approach. Like a politician who has decided the answers she wants give, even before she's been asked the questions, Richard was able to bring all of his responses back to his key priorities for the business, whether he was in a boardroom discussion or talking to a colleague in one of the company's stores.

3. **Expect to communicate it over 6,000 times.** How often do you expect to communicate your strategy? Lets say that your strategy has a 'life' of three years. If you assume that there are circa 200 working days a year and that you have 10 meetings – formal and informal – to share the strategy each day, there are up to 6,000 separate strategy communication opportunities over the three years. As with advertising, it is the frequency and consistency of the message that drives awareness. You might end up becoming bored with saying the same thing in every meeting, but I assure you that your organization will not.

4. **Have conversations, not speeches.** There is a time for major speeches to set out your strategy and vision, but that is just the start, not the end of your communication plan. More important is the drip, drip, drip of your daily conversations. Unless they are in line with your key messages, your carefully crafted annual speech will be quickly forgotten and ignored.

5. **Create an emotional connection, not just a rational argument.** Strong logic and rationale will help your people understand the new strategy, but they will only become committed if there is an emotional impact as well. For example, one of my clients, Avon Cosmetics, focuses its message around its goal of 'empowering women'. This message helps create an emotional connection between the company and its thousands of female representatives around the globe.

6. **Use stories and examples.** One way to create emotional engagement is to use stories. When Sir Stuart Rose became CEO of M&S he used the story of how one product manager developed a new espadrille shoe from idea to the store within 12 days as an example to the rest of the business about pace and effective risk taking. The story brought home to the organization what was important in a way that simple exhortations to act faster simply could not.

7. **Appeal to your people's self-interest.** People aren't afraid of change; they manage change on a daily basis. However, they will only act willingly when it is in their self-interest to do so. You should seek to make a connection with your people's priorities and explain why delivering the company strategy can help them achieve their own objectives. Aligning bonuses and rewards with your priorities are obvious ways of doing this, but there are also other approaches. Appealing to people's desire for personal development and growth, managing your people's wellbeing, increasing the sense of belonging between the company and its people, and demonstrating the wider importance of the work of your organization to society are all factors which have been shown to affect employee satisfaction and loyalty.

8. **Take visible action.** In the end, of course, actions speak louder than words. By taking action consistent with your message, people will see that you are serious; without action your message is just empty words. For example, one way in which P&G's ex-CEO, AG Lafley, hammered home his message that 'the consumer is boss' was by ensuring each of his business trips included in-home and in-store customer sessions.

Can Your Organization Pull This Off?

The final step you should take before signing off on your plans is to ensure that the organization has the capacity deliver it. As we have discussed, you should only be developing solutions that the business has the capability to deliver, but you also need the organizational 'bandwidth' to enable your key initiatives to be implemented effectively. There are three factors that are critical to success for your organization if it is to deliver the strategy effectively.

■ **A critical mass of leaders.** An individual acting alone cannot lead major organizational change and deliver a new growth strategy. As CEO, you are the figurehead for your organization and colleagues across your business will look first to you for direction. However, as soon as they are clear with where you stand, they will immediately look at your fellow executives and other senior leaders across the organization, to see whether or not they share the same vision and priorities. If divisions become apparent, your people will hesitate before committing to the changes you are seeking to make and will be less likely to make the extra efforts that may be necessary or to persevere in the face of the inevitable setbacks.

The coalition-building activities that are necessary to build your leadership team are perhaps most apparent in the world of politics. In her magnificent book, *Team Of Rivals*, for example, Doris Kearns Goodwin sets out how Abraham Lincoln created an environment where the political rivals he beat to become the Republican Party's presidential candidate, and ultimately the US President, were able to work as a team with a shared sense of purpose that remained steadfast in the crucible that was created by the country's civil war. Lincoln gave his cabinet colleagues real accountability over areas of policy, was willing to take the blame for shared failures and, where necessary, played to their individual egos. Lincoln's most difficult relationship was with the Secretary to the Treasury, Salomon Chase. However, in order to create unity, Lincoln was prepared, where necessary, to feed Chase's ego, repeatedly telling Chase and others how critical he was to the future success of the government and the country.

What's clear from Lincoln's story is the need not just to create an initial coalition, but also to nurture and develop it over time. Lincoln's relationships with his team weren't perfect, far from it, but he was successful enough to ensure that Congress continued to provide sufficient support and funding for the war efforts.

- **Technical capability.** We're not all Superman, and we can't always get to where we want in a single bound. Determining your organization's ability to deliver your agenda is critical to the overall success of your strategy. Do you have, or can you quickly acquire the skills and capabilities to turn your big ideas into big results? Again, you need to beware of corporate ego trumping reality. You need to listen to your front-line and technical teams. Keep the pressure on them and demand that they look at options for ensuring that the initiatives are feasible, but you should also be realistic and determine what is actually possible.

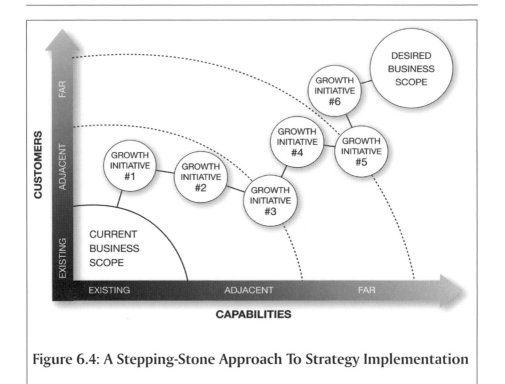

Figure 6.4: A Stepping-Stone Approach To Strategy Implementation

One way to ensure you're making progress, but also keeping in step with your technical capabilities, is to create a 'stepping-stone' implementation plan. As set out in Figure 6.4, rather than delivering your ultimate objective through a single initiative, you may be better off getting there through a series of smaller consecutive initiatives. As you move into these new, adjacent areas, you will pick up the skills, the confidence and the momentum to make the next move less risky and more likely to hit your goals. Rexam, a $7 billion consumer packaging business, for example, transformed itself from a disparate group into a focused packaging business following the arrival of a new CEO, Rolf Borjesson. The transformation did not happen overnight but was driven, over several years, by a series of acquisitions that enabled the company to develop its skills and capabilities in packaging and accelerate its own innovation pipeline.

- **Operational capacity.** Dave Packard, co-founder of computer giant Hewlett Packard once said, *"More organizations die of indigestion than starvation."* In other words, Packard believed that business leaders try to do too much at once, lose focus and become irrelevant. I sincerely believe that most people and teams can achieve far more than they think is possible, and that organizations can get more out of their existing capacity. But this is only possible if they are working to a small, focused number of objectives.

Adding new projects to the 'to-do lists' of managers who are already running at full tilt simply means that nothing gets done very well. As a result, enthusiasm for the new strategy and belief in the leadership team begins to wane, and there is even less chance of success for further strategic projects. Consequently, you should ensure that:

■ *Projects, initiatives and activities that are no longer relevant to the strategy are stopped, killed and killed again!* It amazes me how some projects take on a life of their own, regardless of what's important to the business. A project is not, and should never be, for life. You should review your project list at least twice a year and seriously consider eliminating projects that have been running longer than 12 months.

■ *Your managers have no more than 3-5 key performance objectives.* In my experience it is far better to have people focused on a short set of objectives that are, if necessary, changed two or three times a year, than it is to give them a long list of 10 or 20 'priorities'.

■ *Decisions on how the strategic objectives should be delivered are made as close to the front line as possible.* Companies such as GE have used processes where front-line teams work out for themselves how best to make improvements and deliver their performance targets. That way, there is involvement in the process, ownership of the outputs and a far better chance of unnecessary work being taken out. Whenever front-line managers talk about how they are too busy with the 'day job' to deliver the 'strategy' I know that change is being imposed on them from above and that the organization's delivery capacity is being stretched unnecessarily.

Key Points

- The strategy of many companies doesn't fail in development or implementation, but in the space between these two activities. The strategy gets lost in translation.

- Before starting implementation there are six steps you need to focus on to ensure the organization is engaged and prepared to deliver your strategy: creating genuine alignment, relentless communication, resource allocation, talent deployment and development, setting accountabilities, and agreeing corporate KPIs

- The *Strategy Routemap* can be used as a bridge between your high-level strategy and your detailed implementation and operating plans

- Resource allocation is more effective when you focus on investing in strategies rather than initiatives. Three questions will help you decide what to focus on: Is the initiative critical to your strategy? Is this the most efficient way to fund this initiative? And can you afford the investment?

- You have a critical role as your organization's chief communications officer. You should expect to communicate your strategy at least 6,000 times.

- Your strategy will only succeed if your organization is able to deliver it. This means that it has the leaders in place, the technical skills to make it happen and the operational capacity to focus on the major initiatives.

Chapter 7

THE LAST 98% OF SUCCESS

Like The French Revolution, It's All About Execution

Turning Top-Down Direction Into Bottom-Up Results

Setting a clear strategic direction for a business – identifying the big goals, the critical objectives and the key sources of competitive advantage, and selecting the markets in which you will operate – is the responsibility of the top management team. But delivering the strategy and implementing the actions that will make or break the organization's success is the job of front-line managers and teams. It is a little like oil exploration. The senior engineers and geologists may be able to identify locations that are more likely to have significant reserves, but, in the end, it is down to the drill teams to find a way through the layers of rock to the reservoir of oil.

These exploration teams will undertake the detailed geological studies, structural and seismic investigations and initial drilling to confirm the presence of oil, and other front-line teams will turn proven reserves into actual oil production, with all the risk and complexity of engineering, drilling and distribution that this activity involves. Without the initial identification of a possible or likely oil field, the oil company will not succeed. But this is just the start, the first 2%. The remaining 98% of their performance depends on execution.

This symbiotic relationship between top-down direction and bottom-up execution is critical to any organization's performance. Without direction the individual parts of the business may demonstrate their capabilities, but they will often pull apart creating tensions between different functions. Without effective execution, the company will simply spin its wheels and everyone, particularly the top team, will become increasingly frustrated.

This relationship also provides ongoing learning and development for your organization. Figure 7.1 demonstrates that your 'realized' strategic future is, in the vast majority of cases, different to that which you had originally intended. To put it bluntly, stuff happens.

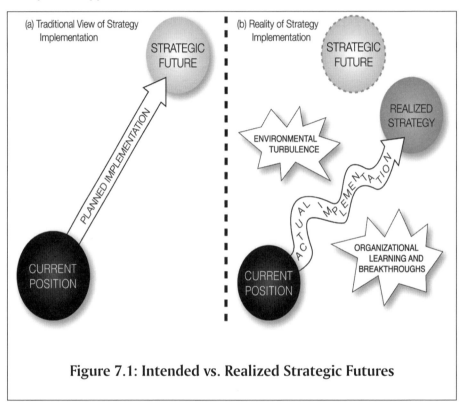

Figure 7.1: Intended vs. Realized Strategic Futures

As you develop and manage your strategy you should not act like some kind of communist state, setting out a 5-year plan and expecting that the organization should deliver it no matter the consequences. Instead, you should view the implementation of your strategy as a dynamic process. A better metaphor is that of a sailor, who knows where she is headed but who will alter the set of her sails to make the most of the winds and who may, at times, alter course to avoid major storms and to take advantage of fast-flowing currents.

This means that you must separate objectives from tactics. If your front-line teams are to deliver the results and meet the objectives you have set, they must be given some leeway to respond to environmental and organizational changes and have the ability to find the best route to success. As we shall discuss later, this is why ongoing performance management of your strategic objectives and regular dialogues with your operating teams are so critical.

Figure 7.1 demonstrates two forces on your organization and strategy that may require ongoing adjustments. Externally, new technologies, changes in consumer attitudes, tastes and needs and economic changes, among other things, can all create the need to review your direction, speed and priorities. In most instances, however, these events and forces do not mean that you should abandon your longer-term objectives. Unless you are a technology business, the emergence of cloud computing, for example, shouldn't mean that you change your overall strategy, but it may provide opportunities for you to manage data without needing to invest in major hardware and systems.

Internally, unexpected successes and failures – your own or perhaps those of other organizations – and changes to your capabilities can demand similar reassessments of direction, speed and priorities. The management of McDonalds, for example, has seen the success of Starbucks and other, copycat chains of coffee shops. After a dalliance with non-strategic investments – the company invested in the UK coffee shop and sandwich chain, Prêt A Manger, for example – the executive team realized that it should determine how it could deliver better quality coffee at a good price within the company's existing operating system, and not simply try to emulate or better the Starbucks offer.

This relationship between top-down direction and bottom-up delivery is reflected in the relationship between strategic focus and the level of organizational opportunism. Figure 7.2 over the page identifies four types of organization based on their attitude and approach to each of these factors.

1. **Failing Follower.** Let's get the weakest position out of the way first. Some companies fail to create a clear strategic focus and yet are also unwilling to jump on opportunities as they arise. These businesses are, in essence, unchanging. Risk-averse and unwilling to try new things until they have been proved elsewhere a million times, they deliver incremental performance improvements at best. At some point, however, they will be overtaken by events and will ultimately decline. Working in these organizations is a little like having a part in the film *Groundhog Day* – each day and each year is pretty much like the last.

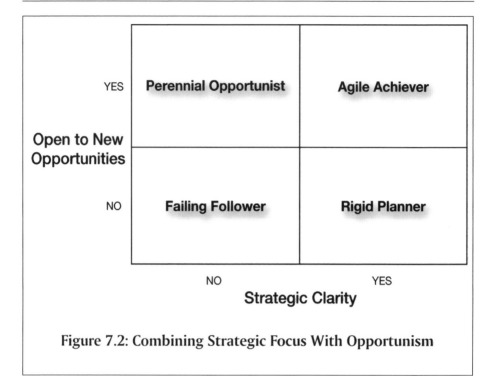

Figure 7.2: Combining Strategic Focus With Opportunism

I once worked with a chain of auto dealerships that was struggling to grow its market share and its profits. One day I was talking to a salesman who told me that he had worked in the business for over 25 years. *"Wow!"* I said complacently, *"You must have seen big changes here over that time."* *"No,"* replied the salesman flatly, *"Not really."* As I looked around his office and saw his manual filing systems, dilapidated desk and chair and worn out carpet tiles I could see that he was right. Change did eventually come to his business: a little over a year later the chain was bought by a fast-growing rival.

2. **Rigid Planner.** Let's be clear, companies that plan well can be very successful. As long as the plans translate into specific accountabilities and responsibilities, and are backed up with relevant resources, things will get done and the ideas you develop for your business have a good chance of being implemented. Developing clearer plans is a key priority for many of the companies I work with. Simply articulating who is doing what and when, and how that will impact both on performance and other teams, provides you with the ability to hold people to account

and enter into a dialogue about how performance can improve. The process of planning also enables you to remove from the agenda those less important projects that can get in the way of the real work that needs to be done. That said, simply focusing on your existing plans can mean that you miss out on new opportunities. A reliance on planning, at the expense of opportunism, is often associated with public sector organizations. But it is also evident in the for-profit sector. One company I worked with started their planning process 9 months before the start of their new operating year. That meant that the finance teams wanted sight of priorities and initial plans 21 months ahead of the end of that operating year!

3. **Perennial Opportunist**. Entrepreneurs are driven by new ideas, and thrive on their ability to turn today's idea into tomorrow's sales. That's fine in very small organizations, but once you reach a certain size, and have to communicate through others to reach everyone in your organization, a complete focus on entrepreneurial activity, particularly that which is outside the company's strategic focus, can be a recipe for confusion, frustration and failure. Some CEOs I work with, however, want to focus solely on immediate opportunities at the expense of the company's long-term direction. They are quickly bored by the detailed thinking that is required to clarify the company's priorities, to allocate resources accordingly and to set up the necessary structures and processes that turn ideas into results on the ground. Instead, driven by their natural curiosity and enthusiasm, they drop new ideas to their executive directors on a regular but ad hoc basis, and then become frustrated when, six months later, little seems to have been achieved. From the organization's viewpoint the CEOs behaviour seems completely unstructured and, over time, they begin to ignore these missives, knowing that 'the boss' will probably change his mind in the next couple of months anyway.

4. **Agile Achiever**. The ideal leader combines a clear strategic focus with an ongoing awareness of new opportunities and a way of incorporating these opportunities into the business. Yes, they have plans, structures and processes in place to ensure that they deliver their strategic goals and objectives, but they also create ways of working that enable them to flex and be responsive to new initiatives without having to start the planning process from scratch. In these organizations the focus

on planning is less important than in the 'rigid planner' organizations. Instead, the key focus is on performance management, understanding what's happening and being open to changes in focus in order to better hit the goals and objectives. They do not develop strategy in annual away days, but in regular monthly sessions, and their executives are willing to shift resources across functions and initiatives in order to meet emerging opportunities. At the start of the financial year, they will have financial goals and plans, but they will also be prepared to actively manage performance, and will add new growth initiatives or efficiency measures, as dictated by changes in the market and their own ongoing strategy development and innovation processes.

Recognizing that successful execution of your strategy requires flexibility as much as it requires planning and performance management, is a critical step in ensuring that your strategy for growth is delivered successfully. But what are the steps you should take to ensure that your key strategic initiatives are set up for success? That is the focus of the next section.

From The Top: Dennis Sadlowski

Dennis Sadlowsk is the former CEO of the US Energy and Automation business of Siemens, the German-based engineering giant. Before a re-organization the business generated $4 billion in revenues and employed 12,000 people across the USA.

Having a clear strategy is paramount to the success of any business. Critically, however, strategy and execution are intrinsically linked. There can be no good strategy that is executed badly. All successful strategies take account of the resources and capabilities that are available to the organization, so that you move forward with confidence rather than merely in hope.

*Linking strategy and execution at the very start of the process
makes it real for everyone and enables the CEO to engage key
executives and managers immediately. I have five lessons for
CEOs to take away from my three-year tenure as the CEO of
Siemens, USA:*

1. **Engagement of the leadership team is critical.**
   *Engagement starts with involvement, and I ensured that the
   executive team and key managers at the next level in the
   organization were intimately involved in the development of
   our growth strategy. We didn't rely on external consultants to
   tell us the way forward; we led the work ourselves, doing our
   own blocking and tackling to make sure we understood the
   detail.*

2. **The strategy must be developed outside-in.** *As an
   executive team, our total focus was on our customers, how
   we were going to be their #1 supplier and how we would
   lead our markets. The internal aspects of our strategy, and
   how we would achieve our objectives, were secondary. We
   started with getting to really know our customers.*

3. **Strategy is as much about behaviours as it is about
   programs.** *Our customer focus meant that I spent significant
   time with our customers, finding out what was important
   to them and what they thought of us. I expected the same
   behaviours from my executive colleagues and our top 200
   leaders. These changes in behaviours embedded our strategic
   priorities far better than any documents, plans or KPIs.*

4. **Pay attention to who's not coming on board and
   address it.** *This is important at all levels, but for the CEO
   it starts with the executive team and the next generation of
   leaders.*

5. Don't mention the word 'change'. *Instead, focus your communication on what the company will achieve in the future, how it will work and what factors will ensure its success. People respond negatively to the word 'change', but are positive about changing if they can see where they're headed.*

The focus on the future, the engagement of the top team and the importance I placed on certain behaviours created genuine alignment. People understood our objectives and priorities and were able to make the right decision on a day-to-day basis. And, in the end, it is these decisions that will determine whether your strategy succeeds or fails.

Ten Guidelines For Setting Up New Strategic Initiatives For Success

This isn't a book about program management, but it's worth spending a little time setting out how you should organize new strategic initiatives that fall outside of 'business as usual' so that you maximise their chances of success. These strategic initiatives are major enablers of your organization's future success that just can't be delivered by line teams on their own. Examples include developing new forms of competitive advantage, large-scale changes to key processes, such as building a new supply chain system, and entering a major new category, geography or distribution channel.

In each of these examples, if operating teams were to lead them without any further support, the team's attention would quickly become focused on more immediate and urgent operating issues affecting the business, and away from the important, but less urgent, task of building future revenue and profit growth.

Instead, a separate, often dedicated team is required either to lead the initiative from end-to-end, or to act as a support team to the operators, helping to facilitate the required changes. Here are my top ten guidelines for making sure that strategic initiatives succeed.

1. *Ensure the program leader has the right capabilities for the job.* I know that this is obvious, but I have seen too many instances where the program leader is totally unsuited to the work demanded by leading a major strategy initiative. Some skills will be specific to the technical nature of the work at hand, but there are also some generic capabilities that are essential to this role. First, the program leader must be a great communicator and networker, and have strong influencing skills. Some people will inevitably feel threatened by changes to their roles, responsibilities and ways of working, and the program leader plays a pivotal role in keeping all the key managers onside and supportive of the program's objectives. Second, the program leader must be highly organized and able to manage multiple streams of work. There is a level of detail that the program leader needs to master to ensure that the program is making sufficient progress. Lastly, the program leader needs to have high self-esteem and demonstrate discipline and persistence. Strategic initiatives tend to involve some level of failure and setback and it's imperative that the leader does not let this destroy his or her confidence or their desire to deliver the results required.

2. *Always take a cross-functional approach.* Few, if any, initiatives that will drive your strategy forward and deliver major business benefits can be delivered through a single function. Ensure that people from across the organization staff your program teams, so that potential issues and obstacles can be spotted and tackled early and that a broader view of the initiative's potential benefits is taken. The product management team at a household product manufacturer I worked with, for example, had been struggling to increase the pace of its innovation and new product development. It was only when the CEO insisted that the product managers worked with managers from manufacturing, supply and marketing that real progress was made.

3. *Create urgency and pace from the 'get go'.* Pace is essential to the successful delivery of change projects, and you must set the standard in the way you behave and make decisions and in the demands you make of your program teams. One CEO I know, newly appointed to the company, wrote to his new executive team with this message: *"We must demand the impossible, set stretch goals and be unreasonable to get the job done. Few people know the limit of their abilities, and we will encourage brevity and simplicity as complexity is the enemy of pace."*

4. *Focus on results.* It's not enough for the program team to deliver the agreed actions if it doesn't produce the results. You must ensure that it is the program's results that people are focused on and not the process. This means that you must have clarity on the business benefits you want the program to deliver. Unfortunately, too many strategic programs I come across have unclear objectives. At a technology company I worked with the executive had defined a small set of strategic challenges for the company to pursue. But neither the CEO nor the executive sponsors were able to succinctly describe the results they required from these challenges. Six months later little progress had been made on any of them, and the program teams, when asked to provide an executive update, focused on the actions they'd taken, not the results they'd achieved. It was only when the CEO and the executive team spent time determining the specific performance improvements they wanted that the program teams began to make real progress.

5. *Wherever possible, start small and learn fast.* Some programs demand major changes from the start. Building a new central distribution centre, for example, demands that you make the full investment up-front. Many initiatives do not have to be managed in this way, however. New product development, improvements to customer service, most process changes and better ways of working can all be delivered by making use of prototypes, trials and rapid testing. This way, you can discover what's likely to work best within a short timeframe – say a month or two – rather than waiting six or twelve months for a grand plan to emerge. In past naval battles the captains fired their first guns simply to get a marker and help the gunners find the best angles and trajectories. You should take a similar approach with your strategic initiatives. Get something out there that you can test, even if it is only in a small focused area, and refine your thinking and approach based on the results you achieve and the feedback you receive.

6. *Communicate the initiative's importance but avoid big stage-managed presentation announcements.* Communicating your strategy is essential, but big set-piece events and strategy 'launches' are unlikely to capture your people's imagination. Many of them will have already lived through other 'grand plans' and, quite literally, have the mugs and t-shirts for previous process redesign, culture change or productivity improvement programs. You are far better off letting people know

what's happening and why it's important, and then rapidly and regularly feeding back to them the results and improvements that the business is delivering. People will believe results over promises every day of the week, and it is the results that you achieve that will sway any doubters you might have.

7. *Integrate the initiative's plans with relevant operating plans.* I am always puzzled by the distinction that some managers seem to make between 'strategic initiatives' and 'the day job'. Part of everyone's day job is delivering the company's agreed strategy. Yet this will only happen if line managers and their teams are properly aligned with the strategy. Failure to do this can be a huge obstacle to securing progress for your major strategic programs. The plans that your program leaders develop for their initiatives should therefore be mirrored by the operating plans your line managers create.

8. *Embed accountability through performance management systems.* You can accelerate and encourage co-operation between your program and line teams by ensuring that specific elements of the action plans and results you're seeking from your key strategy projects are set out in the performance objectives of your line teams. At one of my clients the CEO led a process to cascade the key business objectives that he had developed with his top team throughout the organization. By breaking down each of the high-level objectives into more granular goals, he was able to target specific performance improvements for each of the company's departments and teams. Once that had happened, these teams saw the major cross-functional programs as a way of helping them achieve their goals, rather than as a hassle that would prevent them from carrying out their 'day job'.

9. *Have a direct line of communication with the program team.* As with your line teams, it is essential that you have access to the teams delivering your major change initiatives and, even more importantly, that they have access to you. Even where you set up executive sponsors to lead the work on behalf of your top team, there are times when only the CEO can make the difference. In smaller organizations this is relatively easily done, but in larger companies you will need to make more effort. Despite being almost universally derided for bringing his company to its knees, you can perhaps learn something from Sir Fred "The Shred"

Goodwin, the ex-CEO of UK banking giant, RBS. Sir Fred made sure that he sat on the monthly review of new service ideas that staff from across the bank wanted to put forward for development. Not only did his presence give a symbolic message about the importance of organic innovation to the bank's future performance, it also allowed Sir Fred to interact with the innovation team and learn more about what was most likely to work.

10. *Ensure the initiative has an end date.* There are few things sadder in the corporate world than a program team's office five years on from the program's launch. The (very) few people that visit the office will see plans on the wall that tend to be years, rather than months, out of date and the general air of neglect that surrounds the room reflects the miniscule progress that is still being made. Few strategic initiatives need to last longer than a couple of years, and most can be handed over to your line teams in less than a year. You should ensure that your program leader has a specific objective and milestone to complete the handover to the line and switch the lights off in the program office before the program starts. That way you will encourage simplicity, focus and pace and have the best chance of delivering real results.

From The Top: Ian Filby

Ian Filby is the CEO of DFS Limited, the UK's largest sofa retailer with a turnover of over $1 billion, which is currently owned by the private equity group, Advent.

One of the big strategy lessons I have learnt as CEO of DFS is that a strategy has to meet a clear goal. Without agreement about the goal, you can't settle on your strategy. As a result, one of my first tasks was to agree the exit strategy goal – to agree the size of the business, its growth prospects and the type of sale expected by the owners.

As we did this we realized that we had different sale options according to the length of the current ownership journey, that inevitably would be market dependent.

We then built on these insights to create some new growth options, which hadn't previously been considered. That's what I mean about goals driving strategy.

The other thing I would say about private equity ownership is that the decision-making process is far quicker than I've experienced in publicly quoted companies. In listed businesses, particularly multi-billion dollar corporations, there are many committees that manage decision-making. This multi-layered approach ensures good co-ordination but is inordinately slow.

It is very different with private equity owners. I only have three external stakeholders I need to consider for most of my major decisions. This immediately makes things a lot faster especially as access to them is easy and fast. On top of this, my owners want me to take the lead. Basically, as long as we stay within our financial parameters we are, as a management team, free to do whatever we think is in the best interest of the company and its long-term value.

Reviewing and Managing Progress

I find that many CEOs fall into one of two camps when it comes to tracking progress with major strategic initiatives. In one camp is the *Arms-Length CEO*. These leaders believe that the hard work has been done in creating the strategy and that, since their executive team is made up of fully-grown adults, each executive director should be responsible for tracking and managing their projects' progress. Typically, these leaders prefer the excitement of strategy creation to the – as they see it – administration and bureaucracy of managing delivery.

Overall Status	RAG
What is the level of overall progress and are we on track to meet our goals?	
What's working well and what needs to change?	

Key Issues to Resolve	Decision Required
Issue #1	
Issue #2	
Issue #3	

This Month's Milestones	Status	Comments
Milestone #1	RAG	
Milestone #2	RAG	
Milestone #3	RAG	
Milestone #4	RAG	
Milestone #5 etc	RAG	

#1 Goal	Actual	Target	Status	Comments
GOAL			RAG	

Supporting KPIs	Actual	Target	Status	Comments
KPI #1			RAG	
KPI #2			RAG	
KPI #3			RAG	

RAG stands for Red, Amber and Green. A "Green" status is fully on-track; "Amber" has certain issues, but they should be resolved in the near future; "Red" is off-track.

Figure 7.3: Strategic Programme Update Report

At the other end of the spectrum of strategy management is the *Meddling CEO*. These leaders want daily updates on progress and tend to establish highly intricate systems and processes to track benefits, with a central programme management office team responsible for pulling together executive reports.

Neither of these extremes tends to work too well. The *Arms-Length CEO* fails to embed accountability in his business and the executives can become confused about who's doing what and which initiatives are the most important. Ironically, the *Meddling CEO* also fails to embed accountability into the delivery of the company strategy. In this case, however, the problem isn't a lack of interest, but excessive interest and control. The sophisticated systems and the reliance on a separate programme office simply serve to take the heat off the rest of the executive team.

As with most business management issues, the simplest solutions are generally the best. A monthly executive session that focuses on reviewing the implementation of your agreed strategy and key initiatives is the starting point for review. Not only does this provide a regular focus on progress, but it also provides the executive team with a forum for sharing ideas and reviewing issues outside of the heat and urgency of operational meetings.

The next question is what should the executive team discuss and review in these meetings? I think that there are three elements to these sessions:

1. **Progress review of strategic performance and key strategic initiatives.** Delivery of your strategy is likely to be achieved through a series of programs and initiatives. You must therefore ensure that adequate progress is being achieved, identify and resolve issues and perhaps accelerate delivery if things are going well. You don't need overly complex reports and updates to achieve this. Even in multi-billion dollar enterprises I have found that a simple one-page report, as set out in Figure 7.3, is enough to allow the CEO to ask the right questions and to ensure that the executive leader remains accountable for results. The updates against the agreed plans are a mix of milestones and KPI's and should highlight the issues and decisions required from the CEO and wider executive team. I have found that by spending thirty to sixty minutes spent of focused time on each program each month you can transform the speed and effectiveness with which your strategic objectives are delivered.

2. **Reviews of Key Strategic Issues and Opportunities.** The world doesn't stand still while your programs are being delivered. For most businesses it is not appropriate simply to wait until next year's strategy

process begins before you update your assumptions and understanding about what's happening in the wider world. Instead, you should find ways to review your big issues and opportunities on an ongoing basis. A great way to do this is to take one or two of your major issues each month and spend some time in broader conversation about the latest developments and trends on each of them, identifying the potential implications for your business, and agreeing whether you need to amend your response to them in any way.

3. **Developing new ideas.** The growth of any business starts with an idea. Nurturing and developing these ideas is a critical aspect of any CEO's role. Your monthly strategy sessions are an ideal forum to discuss emerging ideas and for your managers to propose new ways of improving the performance of your organization. At Amazon, Jeff Bezos has implemented a senior leaders' meeting that does this on a weekly basis, supported by bigger, more structured two-day review sessions every six months. The ideas you discuss here may not be so urgent, and may only drive performance in a few years' time. But time spent in a cross-functional forum on your longer-term growth agenda keeps everyone's focus on what's happening in the real world *and* on raising the bar, and helps avoid your team from becoming too incremental and too internally focused.

From Meaningless Quick Wins To Meaningful Milestones' Management

One of the biggest drains on your organization's time and energy are "quick win" projects. These projects often emerge at the end of a team or departmental 'away day'. Following a brainstorm of potential ideas to improve performance, each idea is reviewed on two dimensions: (1) its overall value impact; and (2) its ease of implementation.

Unfortunately, few, if any of the ideas are both high-value and easy to implement. Instead you end up in a discussion over whether to pursue high-value, hard-to-implement initiatives, or lower-value, easy-to-implement projects. More often than not, the low-value, easy-to-deliver projects win out. The barriers to the big prizes just seem too big and too difficult – especially at the end of a long and tiring workshop. But pursuing the "quick wins" is mistaken, for three reasons:

1. *Their impact is too small to register on any performance scale.* This means that the project is never at the top of anyone's priorities and is never delivered.

2. *They consume more effort than you originally estimate.* The lack of progress means that you have to spend more time managing your project and communicating with and influencing your reluctant stakeholders.

3. *They prevent you from getting on with more important projects.* This is the biggest reason of all. As Apple boss, Steve Jobs, once said, *"It's only by saying no that you can concentrate on the things that are really important."*

So how do you ensure that you are focused on actions that are both valuable and strategically important? The simple answer is to get on with the important stuff. If something is valuable, but difficult, that is all the more reason to do it.

Here are three practical steps you can take:

1. **Stop, reduce, slow down, delegate or defer "quick win" projects** that have neither a significant financial or strategic impact. One of the first acts that Sir Stuart Rose took when he became CEO of UK retail giant, M&S was to reduce the number of 'strategic' projects from over 30 to less than ten, so that the energy of the organization could be sensibly focused.

2. **Refocus your time and effort onto high-value projects** that are directly in line with your broader strategic objectives, even if they are harder to implement. As Jeff Bezos, CEO of Amazon, once commented, *"It's important to be stubborn on the vision and flexible on the details."* By this he meant that Amazon's success came from relentlessly pursuing big strategic objectives and being willing to develop and test many different solutions before finding the best one.

3. **Break these projects down into bite-sized chunks**, enabling you to create the focus, momentum and pace that is required to deliver success. This requires that you identify the major milestones the project should deliver, as set out below.

Breaking down projects into chunks is the essence of milestones management. It is, in my opinion, one of the most under-utilized and under-appreciated management tools.

A few years ago, for instance, I completed my first major cycle ride. The Coast-to-Coast route takes you across northern England from Workington, on the west coast, to Tynemouth, on the east. Along with a couple of friends, I covered the 150 miles across a mix of road and off-road routes over the hills of the beautiful English Lake District and the bleak, treeless Pennine moors in three days.

This was a new and exhilarating experience and one lesson in particular has stuck with - the power and motivation of milestones. The weather, particularly on the first day, was horrible – wet, windy (I was blown off my bike twice) and cold. On a glorious summer's day it's easy enjoy the view and be in the moment. When it's lashing down with rain the thought that you are making real progress is essential for your psychological wellbeing.

In today's torrential business conditions using milestones to remind you and your organization that you are still moving forward will be critical to improving your collective momentum and commitment.

Here are five lessons from our bike ride that will help:

1. **Have a crystal clear, ultimate goal.** We benefited significantly from knowing our overall objective (reach Tynemouth). Without such a specific goal we would have given up a lot earlier, and, most probably, have not set off in the first place. *Are your project teams clear on what they are seeking to achieve and what success looks like?*

2. **Milestones must be celebrated – but not always publicly.** I made sure that I celebrated all the milestones in some way. Some were private, such as waiting to open my next chocolate bar until I'd reached the top of a particular climb, or a small group reward, such as stopping for a cup of tea when we reached a particular town, while others were big enough to share more widely. For example, I called my wife after completing the first day's route, and sent texts to my friends after we'd finally reached Tynemouth. *Do your projects have a set of agreed milestones, some for the project team only and others for public celebration?*

3. **Beginning the endeavour is a milestone in itself.** Goethe, Germany's giant of literature, once wrote, *"Whatever you can do, or dream you can, begin it. Boldness has genius, power, and magic in it."* Such magic should be celebrated in some way and we made sure we took group photos at the start as well as at the end of our journey. *Do your project teams celebrate the start of the project and spend time with each other to develop strong social as well as business relationships?*

4. **Don't have too many milestones too early.** I soon learnt that in the first couple of hours it was important not to think too much about milestones. Far from being motivational, they simply reminded me of how much more there was to do. This was the time to simply get my head down and get on with it. *Are your projects' milestones meaningful and demonstrate that real progress has been made?*

5. **Group dynamics are strengthened through shared achievement.** Looking back and seeing how far we had come gave us renewed energy to keep going. Sharing our feelings of success, however insignificant to those outside our small group, helped give us the belief to tackle our future challenges with greater confidence. *Do you find time throughout the project for the cross-functional team to celebrate their progress and achievements together?*

Focus on your big projects, your big wins, not meaningless "quick wins" that will simply become a distraction for your organization. As your teams then break down these major, meaningful challenges into more focused sub-goals and milestones, they will increase their energy, motivation and enthusiasm and accelerate the delivery of your biggest strategic objectives.

Key Points

- Strategy development gets you 2% along the road to success; the other 98% is driven by implementation
- Plans are essential to success, but should be flexible and balanced with a good degree of organizational opportunism
- There are 10 rules for setting up a new initiative for success. These include ensuring the program leader has the right capabilities for the job, always taking a cross-functional approach and creating urgency and pace from the get go
- Focused monthly reviews of your strategic initiatives by the executive team can rapidly accelerate delivery of these programs
- Break down your big initiatives into meaningful milestones, and don't create and pursue meaningless quick win projects that won't help you deliver your strategic objectives

Chapter 8

ARE YOU PULLING TOGETHER OR PULLING APART?

Which Came First, The Chicken Or The Strategy?

Structure Follows Strategy – Only If You Make It So!

At some point in your strategy development process you, or one of your team will ask the question, "*Do we have the right organizational structure to deliver this strategy?*" Very quickly the atmosphere in the room will change. You, and your executive colleagues, are immediately aware of three things. First, it dawns on you that pursuing your new goals, objectives and strategy may not be best achieved through your current structures. New roles, new teams, even new businesses may be required to achieve success, and the people in the room may not be the ideal candidates to lead them. When, in the 1980s, General Motors' management decided they needed to better compete with their Japanese rivals, they set up a totally separate business, Saturn, under the banner of *A Different Kind Of Car Company*. The business eventually stagnated and was shut down by GM in 2010, but early sales demonstrated that this new, greenfield business was better able to understand and meet customers' needs than its organizationally rigid parent company.

Second, you realize that some of your existing structures may no longer make sense. At the very least, your current organization may not be optimally placed to deliver your future ambitions. I was once running a strategy retreat for a household product manufacturer. On the first day the team set out its new goals in terms of sales, profit, target customers and the company's overall level of growth. In short, the team wanted to accelerate product innovation, reduce its time-to-market for new products and have a far bigger share of sales and profits from products developed within the previous three years. At the start of the second day, the manufacturing director put up his hand and said to his colleagues that, given the company's new goals, it may be better to shut down its manufacturing plants and focus on creating a world class product development and innovation center that could work with third party manufacturers to produce goods at lower cost and greater speed.

Lastly, as you contemplate the new organization that may be required to deliver your strategy, you will begin to grasp the scale of change that is necessary. In my previous example the manufacturing director had rapidly grounded the strategy, and raised the bar for everyone else in the room. His executive colleagues began to realize that pursuing their new strategy meant changing the way they worked and being willing to give up on some of the company's historic sources of success. Unsurprisingly, for some executives this process can be far more emotional than it is analytical.

It is for these reasons – the need for new roles and teams, the potential requirement to shut down existing structures, and the difficulty in managing these changes – that many executive teams water down their ambitions. Worse still, they decide to keep the goals, but limit the level of organizational change they are willing to deliver. That is why structure doesn't always follow strategy, and it is a critical reason why many companies' fail to achieve their strategic goals.

So what do you do? At the very least it is your job, as CEO, to make sure that there is a serious and reasoned discussion about the best organizational approach for your strategy. There is not a 'one-size fits all' solution, and you must be willing to make real choices and trade-offs. If you don't, your organization may start to pull in different directions. At the subsidiary of one multi-billion dollar consumer goods company I worked with, for example, the local team had decided it wanted to lead on service, relying on the skills of its local sales team to fulfil the needs of customers. Back in head office, however, the group leadership had decided to focus on convenience as the core of its new strategy. One consequence of that decision was the restructure of the company's manufacturing capabilities, which included the closure of the local team's factory. Instead of being able to control production locally and rapidly ramp up the output of high-selling lines, they had to send in quarterly forecasts to the factory in central Europe, radically reducing their ability to respond to their customers' immediate demands and undermining the strategy that they had settled on.

Strategic Focus	Key Capabilities	Typical Organizational Approach
Product Leader	• Identifying new customer needs and wants • New product development • Brand management and communication • Managing product life cycles	• Cross functional product project teams • External partnerships • Product and brand managers are the key positions
Cost Leader	• Cost management • Cost reduction innovation • Process, technology and management simplification • Productivity improvement	• Highly centralized • Wide spans of control • Few organizational layers • Strong team ethos across operations
Convenience Leader	• Operational and systems management • Systems and process development • Continuous improvement • Cost management	• Process and systems led structures • Emphasis on continuous improvement by front-line teams • Strong team ethos across operations
Service Leader	• Interpersonal and technical skills of front-line teams • Customer service innovation management • Managing customer issues and problems • Service delivery management	• Service standards controlled centrally, delivery management decentralized • High investment in training and development • Recruit for customer empathy first, technical skills second
Solutions Leader	• Develop and deliver bespoke customer solutions • Customer relationship management • Interpersonal and technical skills of front-line teams • Flexible operations and service delivery processes	• Highly decentralized • Local sales and solutions teams are the key players • Emphasis on entrepreneurialism and initiative • Emphasis on sharing knowledge

Figure 8.1: Aligning Structure With Strategy

Figure 8.1 demonstrates that different strategies require different structures and organizational approaches. Here are the five high-level organizational types.

1. Product Leadership

Product leaders are driven and organized around their need to develop new products and accelerate innovation. Companies such as Nike, 3M and many of the pharmaceutical giants are characterized by having a myriad of organic, cross-functional project teams operating at any one time. They may not always be the most efficient organizations, but they will be focused on increasing the speed at which they introduce new products to the market and their impact on market and customer shares. The CEO and the top team are likely to have rapid access to these project teams so that they can quickly identify and back the likely winners.

The key capabilities of product leader organizations are:

- Understanding customer needs – both stated and hidden;
- New product development –its speed, cost and quality;
- Product prototyping and testing;
- Ad-hoc project management;
- Brand management and communication;
- Applying technologies in new and innovative ways;
- Managing product life cycles; and
- Customer segmentation and product positioning and pricing.

The key organizational risk for product leaders is that they fail to manage the efficiency of their innovation processes and that they over-invest in new products that don't deliver a reasonable return. It is critical that there is early focus on identifying likely winners and limiting the investment in those ideas with lower potential. The executive team should also review and manage the time to market of new ideas and the cost of their product development processes.

2.   Cost Leadership

Cost leaders are masters at keeping things simple. These businesses may not have the finest systems in the world, but everyone, following the lead of the owner or CEO, will manage costs to the bone and avoid unnecessary complexity. Cost and productivity measures are the critical performance measures. The organization is likely to be both centralized and flat, and most managers, starting with the CEO, will have wide spans of control and limited support. Rather than using traditional brand communication channels, the company will rely on a stream of PR to get its message across.

The key capabilities of cost leaders are:

- Cost reduction innovation;
- Cost management;
- Process, technology and management simplification;
- Productivity improvement;
- PR management;
- Identifying and exploiting competitors' cost weaknesses; and
- Cost and buying negotiation skills.

The key risk for cost leaders is that they cut costs too far and customers begin to believe that the low price simply isn't worth the hassle. Management must keep a close eye on their target customers' attitudes and behaviors, and ensure that the company's strong value proposition doesn't become a problem. The executive team must also ensure that in its desire to cut costs and offer customers low prices, it can still deliver robust profit margins. The crunch time for many cost leader companies arises when the company becomes too big to use informal management systems and must adopt more formal processes and technologies. Cost leaders can fail when early success and growth demands greater investment that wasn't anticipated in the original business model.

3. Convenience Leadership

Convenience leaders are focused on their systems. As the boss of McDonalds would say, *"We keep our eyes on the fries."* The operating system is central to these organizations' success. For companies such as Wal-Mart, Dell and Amazon new products or services will only be offered if they can be delivered through the company's existing operating systems. Managers and executives are focused on reviewing and managing the cost, productivity and reliability of their core processes and systems.

The key capabilities of convenience leaders are:

- ■ Operational management and performance reliability;
- ■ Systems and process development and management;
- ■ Continuous improvement skills and productivity improvement;
- ■ Team management;
- ■ Cost and price management; and
- ■ Delivery of simple, repeatable added value services.

The big risk for convenience leaders is that their focus on their core systems and processes blinds executives to the need for greater product innovation. During the early 2000s, McDonalds struggled to grow, as they were relatively unresponsive to the health and competitive issues they faced. The executive team and the company responded, however, by improving the level of innovation within the business, in terms of providing a greater choice of healthy options, the inclusion of cappuccino and other coffee drinks, and the improvement of the restaurant environment.

4. Service Leadership

Service leaders are focused on the expert advice and added value support they provide for their customers. The role of the front-line teams in delivering the service proposition is fundamental to these companies' success, and the level of training and development will be high. Managers and executives will be focused on customer satisfaction and loyalty, as much as they are on the financials.

The key capabilities of service leaders are:

- The technical expertise of front-line teams;
- Operational excellence, where it directly impacts on the customer;
- Interpersonal skills of front-line teams;
- Customer service innovation management;
- Managing customer issues and problems; and
- Understanding customer needs.

The key risk facing service leaders is that they put too much resource and cost into the service proposition, diluting their returns. It is essential that management separates those service opportunities that will add real value from those that do little to delight customers. This means that front-line teams must be clear on accountabilities and decision rights so that the speedy resolution of issues is delivered, but that they do not persistently commit to spending where it is unlikely to drive value.

5. Solutions Leadership

Solutions leaders are advantaged by their ability to create bespoke solutions that meet their customers' wider needs. Even more than with service leaders, the front-line teams are the kings of these organizations. The company's executive team will be focused on understanding their customers' level of loyalty, spend and lifetime value. For business-to-business organizations management will also track the value that they have helped their customers to deliver.

The key capabilities of solutions leaders are:

- The ability to develop and deliver bespoke customer solutions;
- Building strong relationships with customers at all levels of the organization;
- The expertise and interpersonal skills of front-line teams;

- Understanding their customers' needs and providing customers with new business insights;
- Flexible operations and service delivery processes; and
- Customer development management, to continually increase the value of their customer relationships.

The key risk that solutions leaders must address is how to ensure that the central operations and service delivery teams are not stretched to breaking point by the solutions that are promised by front-line teams. The company's leaders must also ensure that there isn't excessive duplication of back-office support activities in different functions and geographies, balancing the need for efficiency with the desire for flexibility and responsiveness.

Building the Capabilities for Success

In Chapter 4 we looked at how you can assess the competitiveness of your existing capabilities. The key to future success is not just to continue to refine your existing capabilities, but to understand what capabilities you need to deliver your strategic objectives. What's more, some of your existing capabilities may be less relevant to your future growth.

Once you have settled on your future strategy – both in terms of its scope and your sources of competitive advantage – you need to determine the critical capabilities you will need to establish to enable its delivery. The gap between your existing level of performance on each of these capabilities and the level required in the future will dictate where you need to focus your efforts. You will determine your critical capabilities both from your previous analysis and your review of the organizational requirements of your new, emerging strategy.

Figure 8.2 demonstrates a gap analysis for a fictitious furniture company. In this example, the company had decided that it wanted to expand its existing scope, which focuses exclusively on manufacturing upholstered furniture, to also incorporating dining furniture, as well as improving the company's competitive position on price leadership and convenience leadership.

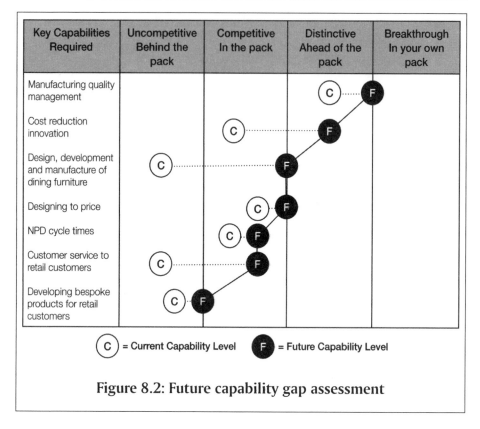

Figure 8.2: Future capability gap assessment

From Figure 8.2, it is clear that the company needs to focus on improving three capabilities to deliver its strategy:

- The design, development and manufacture of dining furniture;
- Cost reduction innovation; and
- Customer service support for retail customers.

The next issue for you and your team to resolve is how you will fill these gaps. In Chapter 9 we will discuss in more detail the opportunities and risks of alliances and acquisitions, but in general you have three broad options:

1. Organic development, focusing on in-house improvements;

2. Partnerships, alliances and coalitions with other organizations; or

3. The acquisition of other organizations.

The solution you select is likely to take into account the level of adjacency of the new capability to your existing skills, the speed of improvement required, and whether the capability is broadly-based, affecting your entire organization, or is relatively isolated in a few areas of the business. In the furniture manufacture example, the company decided to focus on organic development, with focused consultant support, for developing their capabilities in cost reduction innovation and improving their service to retail customers. The executive team considered that the existing operating teams, with some initial guidance, could deliver the level of improvement required. They believed, however, that the acquisition of a dining furniture manufacturer was required to access the skills, assets and capabilities needed to enter this market, working on the basis that this was a relatively big move away from their existing manufacturing capabilities.

Whichever route you take it is critical to treat your capability improvements as you would any other strategic initiative, and that you create a project with clear accountabilities, milestones and performance targets. It is likely that there are elements of capability development in most, if not all, your strategic projects, but ensure that you have sufficient visibility of the improvements in your organization's skills and capabilities so that the changes delivered by your strategic agenda are sustained. I have seen too many projects that have delivered early successes that could not be replicated, because the programs were not set up in a way where the goals and targets were underpinned with real improvements in the skills and capabilities of the organization and its people. Consequently, as soon as the support of the project team was removed from the operating teams, performance quickly returned to its previous levels.

From The Top: Peter Birtles

Peter Birtles is the CEO of the Super Cheap Auto Group of Australia, a $1 billion retail group specialising in automotive parts and care, cycling and outdoors' pursuits.

There are certain things that the CEO must lead in any company's strategy process: setting the targets, signing-off the major investments, and ensuring that there is a robust strategy process. But, over the years, I've found that it's in the informal meetings and interactions where I can actually have most impact.

When I became CEO of the group six years ago, I established quite a formal, and probably rigid, process for our strategic planning. That was fine as far as it went, and the results we achieved were great. Over the years, though, I have realised that even the most confident business leaders will not always share their deepest concerns in large, group sessions.

I was actually leading a strategic planning session earlier today, for example. At one point we were discussing a particularly thorny issue and I could see that a few members of the team were uncomfortable with the way the conversation was going. So, after the formal session, I had a more informal chat with three of the team who felt more able to share their real feelings in a small group session. As a result, we had a much better conversation and reached a better conclusion.

Don't get me wrong, we still need the formal disciplines to ensure that our assumptions are correct and that our plans are properly developed and tracked. But as the leadership team has developed I have found that it is in the less formal meetings and conversations, and my one-to-one sessions with the team, where our key strategic objectives and initiatives are really developed.

The formal planning sessions help us dot the "i's" and cross the "t's", but by being open to my team, by acting as an informal sounding board to them as they're developing their plans, and by building better relationships with each of my executive directors based on mutual trust, we have been able to build a much better, higher-performing business and create a strategy that has delivered against our growth ambitions.

Remember, No Structure's Perfect

There is a level of comfort that many executives find in an organization chart. Once you agree and understand your company's reporting lines you can immediately become more confident about managing and embedding accountabilities. But I think that there is more to it than this. I believe that the mere fact that a structural diagram exists gives business leaders a feeling, often misplaced, that everything will be alright. In an uncertain, ambiguous world, the organization chart provides executives with a feeling of control.

The truth is, however, that even the best structure is filled with weaknesses. Where you push decision-making down to the front line you are likely to gain speed and commitment from your operational teams, which is great, but you are also likely to reduce central control and the ability to co-ordinate activities across functions, channels and geographies. Conversely, a highly centralized structure, with all the decisions made by the top team, ensures control and co-ordination, but does so at the expense of pace and an ability to respond to local circumstances. What's more, you may well find that your teams are not engaged with the business, do not feel able to control and manage their own activities and that a certain level of cynicism exists in your business.

The important thing is that you take the time to review and understand the likely risks of your proposed structures and determine what steps you can take to minimise these risks without adversely impacting on the benefits that your structure will deliver. There are three over-arching steps you can take to improve your chances of your preferred structure delivering your growth ambitions without being weighed down by its inherent weaknesses.

1. *Embedding values and behaviours.* In some respects value statements have become a cliché of corporate life. Given prominence on banners in the HQ reception area, wall charts in office canteens and positioned at the front of your Annual Report, you may believe that people will 'get it'. Unfortunately, that's unlikely to be the case. People don't believe what they read on banners and wall charts; they believe their own experiences. The good news – and the bad news – about your company's value and behaviours is that it starts with you, the CEO. It is your actions and decisions that set the beat to which everyone else will move. If the value of entrepreneurialism, for example, is critical to achieving your goals and overcoming your structural deficiencies, make sure that you react positively to new ideas and that you do not make

the mistake of punishing those who take measured risks that don't quite come off.

2. *Selecting the right KPIs.* Do your performance measures take account of the possible downsides of your organizational structure? For a product leadership business, for example, you may encourage the use of informal product development teams and, as 3M allow, let your people spend a certain percentage of their time on projects of their own choosing. The downside of this structure is that you get lots of activity but limited results. As a result you may wish to track the pace of new product introductions, the percentage sales from products launched in the least two years and the payback of recent new launches. That way you will be focused on the outputs of your strategy and its effectiveness, and not just the inputs.

3. *Telling the right stories.* As ever, it all comes down to communication. What are the stories that you tell others, both inside and outside your corporation, about how to succeed in your organization? Your role as Chief Story Teller not only serves to inspire others but also demonstrates to them what results and behaviours you're really after, irrespective of the structure you have implemented. Stories can bring to life your strategy in a way that PowerPoint presentations are unable to achieve. They lead to an emotional response, not just an analytical assessment, and so are far more memorable. Review your experiences to identify specific examples that highlight your organization at its best. When, for example, Sir Stuart Rose, the former CEO of UK retail giant M&S, wanted to drive greater pace and personal accountability across the business, he told the story of a shoe buyer who responded to Sir Stuart's feedback about a gap in the range by getting the missing products into the M&S stores in less than a week.

In addition to these steps there is one further thing that will help ensure that your structure is fit for purpose: simplicity. Simplicity adds pace, lowers cost and highlights accountability. The costs of complexity can be significant but also difficult to spot. They only become noticeable once you have reduced the level complexity to an absolute minimum. Organizational complexity is like an overgrown garden. Both are a result of neglect rather than design, and, although you may still be able to see some elements of the original intent, the weeds and light-hogging plants slowly but surely stunt the growth and impact of the best blooms.

A certain level of complexity is inevitable – we live in a dynamic, rapidly changing world with sophisticated technologies. Yet, many organizations make this situation far worse by living with unnecessary management layers, fudging decision rights and accountabilities, setting unclear objectives and persisting with inappropriate projects and programs. Take your organization through a periodic simplicity audit and rate yourself against these statements:

1. We have a clear strategic intent that, in simple, everyday terms, articulates how we will succeed.

2. As a management team we have identified a handful of objectives (say, 3-6) that drive our focus and activity.

3. We have crystal-clear accountabilities across the business, and managers are never concerned that they are stepping on someone else's toes.

4. Managers know exactly how to get approval for a new investment or initiative.

5. In a typical week I spend less than a quarter of my time in formal meetings.

6. We have minimised the number of management layers – there is no further room for improvement.

7. Our planning and budgeting process is short, sharp and effective, taking less than three months from start to finish.

8. When a new programme or assignment isn't working it is quickly adjusted or killed – we do not allow problems to fester.

9. I set my team clear objectives, but leave it to them to work out the best way forward. And they act in the same way with their people.

10. In the past six months we have taken big strides in removing unnecessary complexity from our organization.

How many of these statements can you honestly say you agree with? If it's less than eight then, in my experience, your organization will struggle to deliver major programs of change and development. Without clarity and simplicity, your projects and your people simply get stuck in the organizational swamp, and the more they struggle the more stuck they become. If you want pace and action, you first need to clear the swamp – and that means breaking through your organization's functional silos.

Breaking Through the Silos

We all know that in any organization with more than one person there are differences of opinion. As entities grow and the structures become more formal these differences of opinion and approach can intensify and become institutionalized. This is how silos are created, and they can appear in relatively flat structures as well as very hierarchical organizations.

The impact of silo behavior is that different functions act in the best interests of the function, even when that goes against the best interests of the business. I once led a retailer's store development team, where we developed, tested and rolled out new store concepts and improvements. We had a small development team and relied on the support of colleagues across the key functions to deliver the detailed solutions. For nearly two years I felt as if I was banging my head against a brick wall with the buying team as, despite whatever public promises the buyers made, they consistently failed to deliver the changes and improvements required. It was only when the Buying Director was leaving the company that he turned to me and said, *"Stuart, you should know that I've been the blocker to your projects. I thought that they would get in the way of what we're trying to do here so I made sure your plans didn't happen."*

As with many problems created by silo behavior, the Buying Director and his team achieved their aims through passive resistance rather than active disagreement and conflict. Much of the worst silo behavior is insidious and happens below the waterline. That said, there are always signs – some subtle, others less so – that silos may be killing your strategy. Periodically test your organization against the following criteria:

- Cross-functional projects are regularly delayed and fail to hit their milestones;
- Support functions are duplicated across the organization;
- You regularly have to deal with turf battles between your executive colleagues;
- Relatively simple operating decisions are regularly on the executive agenda for discussion and decision;
- It is difficult to get your best people to volunteer to lead cross-functional programs;
- Your operating costs are noticeably higher than your competitors;
- Your business suffers from the cost of poor quality; and
- Customer information and intelligence is not systematically or regularly shared across relevant teams.

The key to minimizing the negative impact of silo behavior – I'm not sure that you can ever eradicate it – is to focus on the positive actions you need to take and embed in your organization. There is no magic pill solution. Instead, you need to look at this as you would a diet and exercise regime. Once you fail to keep up with your regime you will find, over time, that the symptoms will return. Here are 12 specific actions you can take to break through your organization's silos.

1. *Ensure that you and your executive colleagues model the behaviors you want.* You must exemplify your desired behaviors. Be very specific with your executive team about what you expect from them and hold them to account. Ensure that the executive team is rewarded on the entire organization achieving its goals, and not just their ability to deliver their own function's objectives. *Are your executive directors' bonuses based on them achieving a narrow set of objectives within their departments, or on their role in delivering the company's broader strategy?*

2. *Develop a culture of openness and trust.* Ed Catmull, the founder and president of Pixar, once wrote in the *Harvard Business Review,* "Everyone must have the freedom to communicate with anyone." This also means that everyone must be prepared to receive feedback from anyone. At Pixar any director can call a meeting of his or her peers to show what they're up to, ask for assistance and get their feedback. The directors' ability to accept this feedback is based on a history of mutual trust; each director knows that it's better to get the feedback from colleagues than critics and audiences, and they also know that the other directors want them to succeed. *How often do your managers and executives seek direct feedback on their trickiest issues from their peers?*

3. *Get closer – much closer – to your customers.* When he was CEO of Procter & Gamble, AG Lafley would spend one or two days each quarter in consumers' homes, watching them go about their daily activities and use P&G's and their rivals' products. You can bet that Lafley's colleagues acted in a similar way. The more you and your team are focused externally, on identifying and meeting the needs of your customers, the less insular and territorial they will become. *What percentage of your time do you spend directly with your customers?*

4. *Clarify program leadership accountabilities.* The leaders of your cross-functional programs and projects must know that they are the ones accountable for delivery of the program, and that they can't pass that

accountability to others. One of my clients was running an operating board meeting where an executive director complained that he was waiting for a colleague in another department to deliver a certain action before he could hit a key milestone. The CEO told him pointedly and publicly that he was the one accountable and he couldn't avoid that. The CEO's intervention raised the quality of the discussion and the issue was quickly resolved. *Are you clear about who is accountable for delivering your key strategic programs?*

5. *Co-locate program teams.* Wherever possible, bring cross-functional program and project teams together to deliver your major new initiatives. Co-location helps build communication, trust and team development, enabling the team to focus on achieving the program's key goals rather than simply protecting each function's perceived best interests. *What mechanisms have you established to enable cross-functional project teams to work together effectively?*

6. *Reward cross-functional behaviors.* Promote and publicly reward those who are both individually effective *and* who can build and manage productive relationships across the organization. Let people know that their demonstrated behaviors are a driver of that individual's success. Once people can see that it is likely to be in their best self-interest to act in a cross-functional manner, their behaviors will change relatively quickly. *How important are cross-functional behaviors in accelerating the progression of your top talent?*

7. *Embed cross-functional career development.* Traditionally, many careers happen in a straight line. People join a certain function and then continue through the layers to, hopefully, their level of technical, management and leadership competence. Giving your people experience in different functions, however, can better develop your management talent for the longer term. Their experience in different roles gives them a far better appreciation of the organization, encourages them to work more cross-functionally and be less loyal to specific functions, and, in the end, helps ensure that your customers are served with better, more relevant solutions. *What experience have your top team had in different functional roles?*

8. *Train the behaviors you're after.* There is a role for formal training and development of the behaviors you want. Relationship building and

management, influencing and communication, and meeting facilitation, for example, are all learnable skills that are likely to help your people work more cross-functionally and help break down your organization's silos. *What specific personal development activities do you have in place to help your people improve their ability to work across functional silos?*

9. *Undertake periodic process reviews.* Some corporations, particularly those competing on convenience leadership and cost leadership, tend to be structured around processes. Even where you are not structured in this way but are, say, organized around customer groups or product categories, you should periodically review the effectiveness of your key processes. In addition, if you haven't done so already, ensure that your support and back-office functions are, as far as possible, built around key processes to improve efficiency as well as helping to reduce silo behaviors. *When did you last review the efficiency and effectiveness of your key cross-functional processes?*

10. *Introduce cross-business mentoring.* Encourage your executives and senior managers to mentor your up-and-coming managers in other functions, so that these individuals develop new perspectives and have a more rounded view of the business. *Who do your emerging managers seek out to get independent and objective feedback on their personal impact and behaviors?*

11. *Establish regular front-line reviews with cross-functional teams.* GE established its 'Workout' program to enable cross-functional problem-solving, idea development and performance improvement by self-managed teams. Certain manufacturers, following the example of successful Japanese enterprises, organize daily meetings between workers from various departments to ensure that problems are resolved as quickly as possible without the need to send them up the line to supervisors and managers to resolve. *How often do your front-line teams sit down with colleagues from other functions to review the performance of key operational processes and identify opportunities for improvement?*

12. *Implement knowledge management systems.* I have purposefully kept this as the last point. Knowledge management is a critical element of cross-functional working and silo busting. But it only works once the culture and behaviors are in place that will support it. Your IT team may have access to some great software that will promote the sharing of

information, insights and knowledge, but I would save your money until you see some of the other actions you're taking are having a positive impact on the organization. *What opportunities does your organization have to better and more manage and share key customer insights and operational best practices?*

Key Points

- Delivering a major shift in your strategy may not be possible with your current structure, and you may need a new organizational model
- Each of the five competitive strategies has a different organizational focus and approach that is likely to work best for the business
- As you develop your organization focus on identifying, building and enhancing the capabilities that are most likely to help you achieve your growth objectives
- Remember that no structure is perfect. Embedding the appropriate values and behaviors is even more important to the execution of your strategy than getting the reporting lines right
- When in doubt, ensure that your organization errs on the side of simplicity
- Eradicating the functional silos that inevitably occur in all organizations requires an ongoing focus, but there are practical steps that you can take

Chapter 9

ACCELERATING GROWTH THROUGH ALLIANCES AND ACQUISITIONS

As the U2 song goes, "Sometimes You Can't Make It On Your Own"

What Is Your Company's Natural Limits To Growth?

We have already covered the imperative for you to drive new growth and to continuously evolve your business. Even if you are successful – perhaps especially if you are successful – you will begin to stagnate and fall behind if you continue to rely on yesterday's solutions to meet tomorrow's customer needs. High-performing companies use their current success as a springboard to even further growth. They continue to reach out, creating new products and services, finding new customers and entering new geographies and channels. For some companies, particularly those with a very focused business model and customer offer that operate in large markets such as the USA, it can be possible to simply replicate and extend their offer and grow completely organically. For most businesses, however, the stretch into new markets and geographies will demand, at some stage, that you get help and seek to use the assets and capabilities of other organizations.

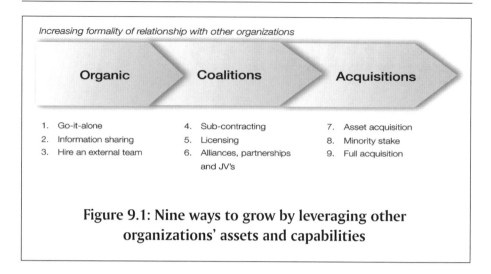

Increasing formality of relationship with other organizations

Organic	Coalitions	Acquisitions
1. Go-it-alone	4. Sub-contracting	7. Asset acquisition
2. Information sharing	5. Licensing	8. Minority stake
3. Hire an external team	6. Alliances, partnerships and JV's	9. Full acquisition

Figure 9.1: Nine ways to grow by leveraging other organizations' assets and capabilities

Figure 10.1 sets out nine different ways that you can grow on the back of others' efforts, accelerating your ability to achieve your strategy and goals. It's likely that your company will be using several of these tactics, and possibly all of them, at any one time, but each offers you a different balance of risk and return. Let's take each of the 9 approaches in turn.

1. **Go-it Alone.** Even where you choose to do everything in-house, you can still use others' efforts to help you accelerate growth. Arms-length benchmarking, for example, enables you to review other organizations' activities and identify areas for where you can learn and adapt. This is especially useful if you are still in catch-up mode with your competitors, or if you are seeking to introduce a business model that is successful in one geographical market into another. Michael O'Leary, for example, studied Southwest Airlines' low-fare model and used it as the basis for Ryanair's business in Europe. High-tech companies can also go-it alone through others, and since the 1960s Japanese companies such as Sony have identified and picked up generic technological breakthroughs, such as transistors, that were first created in the west, before turning them into customer-focused products.

2. **Information Sharing.** A step above arms-length benchmarking is information sharing. This is a slightly more integrated exercise where management teams from different companies agree to host and share certain information and insights about their company, usually as part

of a reciprocal arrangement. When I led the strategy team at Boots in the UK, we entered into such exercises with leading companies from the UK, Europe and North America. We didn't get access to specific assets or these companies' top secrets, but we did gain insights into better ways of managing certain operations that enabled us to speed up certain trials and implementation initiatives. You are, of course, likely to receive a more positive welcome from organizations where you are not in direct competition. That doesn't mean you can't target companies in the same or similar industries. In fact, finding similar businesses that operate in different geographical markets can be a great way to identify new sources of growth and understand the best ways to secure them.

3. **Hire A Team.** Many investment banks, consulting businesses, insurance companies and solicitors' firms cherry-pick high-performing players and teams from rival firms as their way into a new service line. For these knowledge-based businesses, where the key capabilities and assets are the people, this is often the quickest and most effective way to enter a new market. Hiring people with specific relationships and knowledge can also work for sales organizations and technology-based companies. People may not be able to bring patents, brands and manufacturing operations with them, but they can bring their knowledge and experience, helping you to avoid learning everything afresh.

4. **Sub-Contracting.** The downside of hiring is that you may not get the ongoing learning from the company you're hiring from, or the possibility that you hire the wrong person! Sub-contracting services into your business enables you to sustainably and relatively flexibly use the capabilities of another organization to aid your growth strategy. Many corporations use third party sales distributors in overseas markets, particularly where the size of the market is insufficient to justify an in-house team. Similarly, many retailers use companies such as FedEx, UPS or DHL to manage the logistics of their on-line businesses, providing them with a reasonably low-cost, low-investment entry into a new sales channel. Where it works best, sub-contracting becomes a quasi-partnership, with the two parties working together to develop new and better solutions, jointly investing in future growth opportunities.

5. **Licensing**. The decision to invest in a new market or channel is a balance of risk and reward: you want to receive the maximum reward for the minimum risk. Licensing and its variants, such as franchising, reduce your return but also lower your risk. In short, these approaches allow you to receive an income from the assets, brands and capabilities you have built without needing to invest and manage all the requisite operations. Pepsi, for example, licenses several of its key brands to Britvic in the UK. Britvic gains access to a leading brand to drive its growth and relationships with key retailers and distributors in the UK, while Pepsi receives an income without the need to invest in expensive bottling and supply chain operations. McDonalds uses a franchise model to drive its growth. Again, it receives a share of each restaurant's income without needing to provide all the necessary capital or manage the detailed operations. Franchisees, on the other hand, can use the McDonalds brand to develop their own business growth.

6. **Partnerships and JVs**. With most markets encountering rapidly changing technologies and customer tastes, it can pay to work with other organizations to develop new solutions and offers, sharing both the risks and the returns. High-technology industries have embraced the need for collaboration of initial product development for a couple of decades at least, often in broader coalitions rather than simply an arrangement between two of the players. This approach is now being replicated in other industries. Citroen, Peugeot and Fiat, for example, combined their resources to produce their MPV offerings. The body and chassis of their different brands are the same, it is only the internal fit-out that changes. If you wish to enter new, high-growth markets such as China and India you will have no choice but to partner with a local company, but such a move can pay dividends in other countries as well, giving you access to local knowledge and relationships, at least in the early stages of your expansion.

7. **Minority Stakes**. Acquiring 10%-30% of a company can give you the opportunity to gain new knowledge about its business and markets as well as providing you with options for future returns should it become highly successful or you wish to take a bigger investment or outright ownership. Again, minority stakes are popular with high-technology companies, and all the major players are highly active investors in

smaller start-ups. Not only do they hope to find a future winner, but their involvement can also give them a seat on the board, allowing management to build better relationships with the company and invest in certain alliances and partnerships.

8. **Asset Acquisitions**. It is common among consumer goods' companies to buy and sell brands, as the growth strategies of the different businesses adapt to changing priorities and circumstances. These brands often come with sales and operating teams, but they are not necessarily full company acquisitions. Similarly, you could acquire a factory, supply chain, patent or trademark from other companies to help you drive new levels of growth for your business. Towards the end of the 2000s, for example, several of the world's major grocery chains – Tesco, Carrefour, Casino – bought and sold their stakes in various Asian markets to reflect their emerging priorities and their ability to obtain a leading position in each of the countries in which they had invested.

9. **Full Acquisitions**. Full or majority acquisitions give you all the returns for all the risk. You have full control over your new company and how you will generate new value from your investment. *Caveat emptor* is the key phrase for acquisitions as research shows that, for the majority of deals, it is only the selling shareholders who end up actually making money. That said, as we shall see in the following section, you have the opportunity to generate material new value if you follow certain guidelines.

These nine approaches to leveraging the resources and capabilities of other companies to accelerate your growth demonstrate that you do not simply need to decide whether or not you wish to acquire another business: the alternatives are far broader than that. The decision you make will reflect your appetite for risk, the returns available and your specific growth objectives. Full acquisitions and partnerships perhaps provide the greatest opportunity for you to leapfrog the competition and take your business forward. Let's look at each of them in a bit more detail.

Acquisitions That Generate Value, Not Heartache

The corporate world is littered with the wreckage of failed mergers and acquisitions. Like shipwrecks at the bottom of the ocean, these failures act as a warning to other businesses seeking to sail these seas. The generally received wisdom is that two-thirds of acquisitions fail to generate a return for the buyer. I don't know whether that particular statistic is accurate, but you only need to look at the disastrous mergers between AOL and Time Warner, Vodafone and Mannesmann or Chrysler and Daimler Benz to see that it's incredibly difficult to generate value between the merger of two giant organizations and incredibly easy to over-pay, overstate the benefits and over-reach yourself in your desire to make a deal happen.

Take the acquisition of Snapple by Quaker Oats in the 1990s. Attracted by Snapple's high growth and buoyed by the success of its purchase and integration of Gatorade, Quaker Oats paid a staggering $1.7 billion for the up-and-coming drinks brand. Unfortunately Quaker Oats bought at a time when other beverage manufacturers, including Coca-Cola, were bringing out rival brands to Snapple and when consumers' taste for the brand had already reached its zenith. In addition, Snapple had grown through its distribution to local and independent retailers, and the company found it much harder to gain share with Quaker Oats' major customers, the large grocery chains. Just a couple of years later Quaker Oats sold Snapple for $300 million, a loss of over $1 billion.

Snapple may be an extreme example of how acquisitions can create shipwrecks of corporate performance, company reputation and senior executives' careers, but it is far from being an isolated example. Yet mergers and acquisitions continue to be a popular route to growth for many businesses – and there have been sufficient numbers of companies that have used acquisitions successfully to make it an alternative that you should consider. GE, for example, has grown and delivered shareholder value through a myriad of acquisitions, as has the UK construction and support services company, Carillion.

Successful acquisitions are strategy-led. That may seem obvious, but it is critical to driving value from any purchase you may make. Acquisitions work when you are clear on your strategy, business model and growth priorities and can clearly understand how the acquired company will help you achieve one or more of your strategic objectives. That said, many executive teams love acquisitions. Not only are they exciting in themselves, but they can also hide underlying performance issues within existing businesses. You must avoid the temptation to use acquisitions as a plaster to your corporate wounds. History tells us that if you buy for the wrong reasons you are likely to live to regret your decision.

There are two broad reasons why you may decide to buy another company:

1. **Create scale efficiencies.** This has been Carillion's number one
   acquisition objective. From 2005 it bought other construction
   companies, including rivals Mowlem and Alfred McAlpine, helping
   the company to increase its reach and scale and remove duplicating

back-office activities and management. The result was annual increases in earnings per share and shareholder returns in advance of the FTSE indices. Through its acquisitions Carillion has been able to support its organic growth ambitions, but its key route to generating returns from its purchases has been cost-cutting and margin improvement.

2. **Provide access to new growth opportunities**. The alternative route to value generation is to acquire another company that has a set of specialist skills and capabilities that will complement your existing business, and enable you to develop new products and services, reach new customers and enter new markets. Disney's purchase of Pixar, for example, gave Disney access to Pixar's ability to create innovative computer animation movies, and allowed Pixar to benefit from Disney's brand and reach to generate even greater value from its productions. The acquisition was a natural step for the two companies, following their previous alliances and production partnerships.

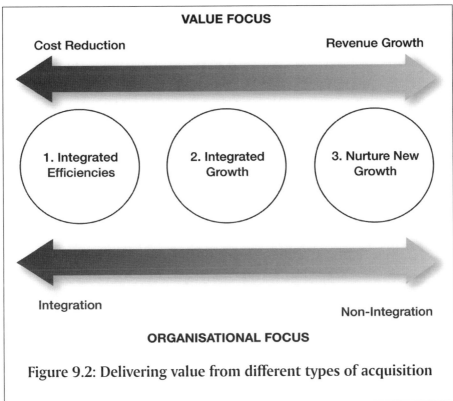

Figure 9.2: Delivering value from different types of acquisition

Before you acquire a business, however, you must also be clear about whether and how you will integrate the new business into your existing operations. As set out in Figure 9.2 there are three broad approaches you can take:

1. **Integrated Efficiencies.** Where you are seeking to gain scale efficiencies it is essential that you rapidly and determinedly integrate the new business – management, systems, processes – into your existing operations. This means that you must ensure that you have a set of goals and plans, often driven by a 100-day plan, to merge the purchased company into your own business. Typically, you will use a small central team, working with divisional and local executives, to ensure that your systems are quickly embedded in the new organization and that operations are managed effectively.

2. **Integrated Growth.** In this situation you will again set out a focused integration plan, but the emphasis will shift to driving new growth across the business. You may gain efficiencies on certain back office activities, but your real value is generated by your new enlarged organization exploiting the new skills and capabilities of the acquired company. This approach works best where the acquired company has specialist skills that are immediately relevant to other parts of the business. The UK-based defense and security business, BAE Systems, rapidly integrates its acquisitions into the group's broader operations with a view to adding to its range of solutions for its global customers.

3. **Nurture New Growth.** The third approach you can take is to keep your new acquisition relatively independent of your existing operations. You may share some common systems, but the new organization will maintain its own identity, culture and ways of working. This solution works best where your acquisition has specialist skills that are still in development and that are relatively distinct from your core business. Over time you may increase the level of integration, but the key job of the parent company in the early stages is to provide funding, support and access to new markets for your acquisition.

Whichever route to generating growth and new value you choose, there are some rules and guidelines for ensuring that your acquisitions join the short-list of successes, rather than the long-list of failures.

1. **Eschew ego-driven acquisitions.** This follows on from the need to ensure acquisitions are strategy-led. You must set and stick to rigorous hurdle rates and performance management targets to ensure that you and your management teams do not pursue needless acquisitions. It is easy to get carried away with the emotion of a new acquisition, but if you're not careful you can convince yourself, if not all your shareholders, why a bad acquisition could make great commercial sense. Ego and emotionally-led decisions are most likely to be made in the following scenarios:

   ■ Your current trading performance is relatively weak, and you need revenues to bolster your ability to hit your targets;
   ■ You are losing ground to the number one player in the market and there is a possibility of a deal with another weaker competitor;
   ■ There is a big potential prize from the acquisition, but the risks of delivering it are also high;
   ■ It would be a big deal in your sector and would create a lot of buzz in your market and possibly beyond;
   ■ You personally stand to make a lot of money from the deal.

   I'm not saying that you shouldn't do deals in any of these scenarios, but you should ensure that you receive and listen to advice about the commercial realities and rigorously test your assumptions about how you can create new profit growth. For integration-led deals, a reasonable rule of thumb is to ensure that you can deliver the returns you're after through cost synergies alone, enabling any growth-led benefits to be the icing on the cake rather than the whole cake itself.

2. **Successful acquisitions require senior leadership.** Alongside a clear strategy, you must ensure that there is real leadership to drive the benefits you have set out in your business plan. Business unit management teams are, in general, cautious. Strong, focused leadership can cut through these issues – in ways that 'programme offices' just can't – to release the targeted value quickly. You will need to spend real time yourself on major acquisitions. For smaller purchases make sure that the leader has sufficient authority and respect across the organization to make things happen.

3. **$1+1 = 7$ or more.** There is a balance between stretch and hubris in setting goals from acquisitions, but rules of thumb are:

   - If you really stretch, you may just surprise yourself. You can manage external expectations downwards, but make sure you have clarity and alignment internally about what success looks like and drive to deliver what you have targeted.

   - To have a chance of getting to "7", you must have a roadmap. Without focus, clear accountabilities and persistence you will never achieve the higher end of the benefits that you've identified. That is why 100-day plans are so helpful in creating pace and momentum into post-acquisition merger activities.

   - The better the price you pay, the more room for manoeuvre you give yourself in driving the benefits of integration. Your ability to create value from your acquisition is generally determined by the price you pay. Use your lower estimates of value growth to determine what you can afford to pay, not your most optimistic forecasts, and always be prepared to walk away if the price isn't right.

4. **People issues are critical to ultimate success.** Even in Cost Reduction Integration purchases, effective involvement and management of people is fundamental to driving value. The acquired business will only become effective for the parent when it can operate in line with the culture and management approach of the group, and that demands leadership from the acquired organization's executive team. In some cases the top team of the acquired company will quickly leave the new group, but even so they must be in a position to tell their people why the acquisition is in the best interests of that company. In growth-led acquisitions you are often acquiring key people as much as you're acquiring particular assets. Managing and securing the ongoing commitment of these key individuals is critical to delivering the value growth you have identified.

5. **Very small deals only work when they are truly a 'bolt-on'.** There is a lot of discussion that mega-mergers don't work, but very small purchases can also be loss-makers. Acquiring a small business can be just as time-consuming as acquiring a larger organization, and, post-acquisition, can become a huge management distraction if it requires significant central support. Overall risk is higher for small deals, as smaller businesses tend to be driven more by personal networks than

by replicable systems and processes. If the potential returns of the acquisition are not particularly material you may be best advised to ignore it unless you are confident that it can be integrated immediately and seamlessly into your existing management systems.

6. **Beware of bringing in banks too early**. Banks can be great for sellers in creating a market and providing distance between the seller and prospective buyers. For buyers, however, banks can create a distraction, as they may be working to their own, rather than the buyer's, agenda. It is better to use a limited number of trusted advisors, and that means investing in a few relationships with key people over a number of years, rather than picking up the phone to listen to every opportunity that may be out there. Again, it all starts with having a clear strategy and route to growth, and understanding what potential purchases will best help you achieve your objectives.

From The Top: Andy Ferguson

Andy Ferguson is the Managing Director of Boots Opticians, the UK's second largest chain of opticians, with annual sales exceeding $500 million. Andy was previously Managing Director of the D&A opticians' chain, and led the merger of the two companies in 2009.

How important was the merger between D&A and Boots to both companies' growth ambitions?

The merger came about because both companies needed scale to challenge the dominant share of the market leader. Both organizations shared the same values, which made the merger much easier, and colleagues in both businesses could see the rationale for uniting behind the Boots Opticians brand. We have adopted a 'better than both' approach and although we recognize both companies' heritages we are not precious about them and have focused our activities on what we need to do to grow the business.

How have you transitioned from managing the integration of the two businesses to creating an integrated strategy for growth?
We haven't seen these as two separate workstreams. From day one, we created our mission and purpose for the business so that all of our transformation activities, both customer facing and business processes, could be set in the context of our ambition for the long term success of the business and recognizing the need for substantial change to get there. Time has helped inform the reality of where we are and where we can go. We have continued to refine the strategy as we have gone along and, as we deliver the business process changes, we have become increasingly able to focus on doing a better job for customers and on creating the new Boots Opticians brand.

How would you describe your approach to strategy development?
I always think about customers, colleagues, competitors and capability. What do customers want and what insight do we have that would give customers reasons to choose us over our competitors? What are our competitors doing, where are they heading, and is there anything that they are not good at that is important to customers? Colleagues will always know what the company is capable of doing and what would feel right for them and their customers if we were to change. In a service business, their belief is everything. They have got to 'get it' in order to have the desire to go the extra mile for their customers.

What are the big strategy lessons you've learned as a CEO?
The biggest lesson is to keep it simple so that everyone in the business can remember what the strategy is. The important thing here is *"the everyone"* bit. Strategy is not for the senior team alone.

Partnerships, Alliances and Growth

Alliances, partnerships and joint ventures may appear to be less risky than acquiring other companies. After all, you do not have to lay out all the money up-front or take on another organization's people and operations. This may be true, but alliances and partnerships take time, commitment and skill to deliver positive and profitable results. I have taken part in partnerships and alliances between two companies where, despite a positive start, the relationship quickly falls apart and the performance of the joint project deteriorates. Like many marriages, you may initially believe that your partnership is a match made in heaven. Even so, you may find that some form of "prenuptial" agreement will help set expectations up-front. There are five criteria that you should use to ensure that your alliances, partnerships and joint ventures are effective, and you shouldn't go ahead unless all five are in place.

1. **All parties have a strong belief in the value of partnerships.** There will always be problems and issues in any alliance. If you or your potential partners are less than sincere in your absolute belief in the value of partnerships those problems will turn from slightly choppy waters to enormous tidal waves of destruction. It's human nature, perhaps, to want to control events and to have all the good ideas, but in a partnership you need to be willing to give the other party the credit and the control where this is in the best interest of the project. This can only be done in organizations that see alliances as a critical route to growth and success. You should ask yourself whether your potential partner really believes in partnerships. Are partnerships, for example, one of their core values and have they demonstrated that value in previous relationships and projects? No matter how attractive the project may appear, if you cannot answer, "Yes" to these questions you shouldn't pursue the alliance.

2. **There is a good fit of senior personalities**. For the alliance to succeed you need to be able to create and maintain strong relationships at various levels between the organizations, but, critically, there must be a good fit and chemistry between the two leaders. Other players in each team inevitably take their lead from the boss, and if the leaders are working well together and getting on it makes it significantly easier for everyone else to work towards the shared aims. You needn't all be bosom buddies, but there should be sufficient mutual respect and trust at the top to enable the project teams to deal constructively with any

175

setbacks and problems as they arise, without an immediate blame game emerging.

3. **Aligned objectives**. All the partners of the coalition must be materially better off from being part of the alliance than not. This means that all parties must be clear on their specific, tangible objectives and, at the same time, recognize and support the objectives of their partners. A partnership cannot function with a win-lose mentality; it must be a win-win. Its success is based on each organization's needs being met. Either all the partners win, or none of them do. Many supplier-retailer relationships, for example, are confrontational and transactional, even when they are nominally called partnerships. This is because both parties are trying to improve their position at the expense of the other. The best, longer lasting relationships are those where each party is working to help the other succeed and achieve their objectives. No relationship is perfect and you will, in the end, put your own organization first, but this shouldn't be at the expense of your partners.

4. **Plan upfront for success and failure**. All partnerships set off together with the firm intention of succeeding. The reality is that some do and, unfortunately, some don't. It is critical that you establish what constitutes success and failure up front, and that you are clear on the consequences of both events. In terms of failure, it is worthwhile thinking through all potential downsides and determining how you would resolve them. Similarly, you should be clear on what success might mean both for this project and potential future joint ventures. I was once involved in a partnership project where the two organizations knew what success looked like, but hadn't agreed how they would share that success. Although the project created new value the bickering over the share of profits enabled the two businesses to snatch defeat from the jaws of victory. Spending time and effort up front to agree this would have prevented much wasted time and investment later on. After all, if you can't resolve your differences up front, it's unlikely that you'll be able to sort them out when you are in the heat of the project.

5. **Create formal ways of working**. The initial teams may be driven by shared enthusiasm and great working relationships, but it's likely that the composition of the teams, including the leadership, will change

over time. You must be able to deal with these changes without needing to start the relationship from scratch. You should therefore create the governance structure for effective ongoing communication and decision-making. This structure is likely to include regular operational review meetings, where all parties can jointly assess and manage progress and performance, and more infrequent senior strategy reviews. These formal channels of communication should build on the informal networks that you develop, but are critical in ensuring continuity of the relationship and in recognizing and resolving issues and threats to the project.

Selling Non-Core Businesses, Not The Family Silver

If you live in the UK you will probably recognize the name, Whitbread. For most people it will conjure up images of warm beer and busy pubs. The Whitbread Company was established in the eighteenth century and became the UK's first mass-production brewery. For over 200 years it brewed and distributed its eponymous ales. Unsurprisingly, the UK's beer drinkers immediately link the word "Whitbread" with "beer". The only problem with most people's image of Whitbread is that the company no longer brews beer or owns and runs pubs. The company still has some pub-restaurants but the key businesses of the group are now Costa, the UK's largest coffee shop chain and Premier Inn, the UK's largest hotel chain. The Whitbread brand and brewing business was sold to Interbrew in 2001, when the company's management realized that they were unable to deliver market-leading returns in this challenging sector.

As we have repeatedly discussed, strategy is all about focus. At some stage that may mean that cherished aspects of your business and brand may no longer be relevant, and that they have become of greater value to you as an asset to sell than to keep. Whitbread may have moved out of its heritage business, but the company was not selling the family silver in some sort of fire sale. Instead, the disposal of its traditional businesses was the result of hardheaded, strategic thinking about the best future for the business. There are five factors that might indicate that you are better off selling part of your business than continuing to manage it yourself.

1. **The business no longer fits with your strategy.** The most obvious reason to sell a business is that it is no longer a good strategic fit. Using the *strategy arrow* we described in Chapter 3, if the business no longer meets your playing field or how you will win, you should consider disposal. It is likely that another business is likely to make more money

from it than you will, and they will therefore be willing to pay a price for it that is of greater value than if you kept the business in-house. As consumer goods businesses refine their strategies they regularly dispose of non-core brands. Sara Lee, for example, sold their personal care business to Unilever in 2010 as part of the company's increasing focus on its food and beverage brands. In 2011, the company went one stage further and announced that it would split the company into two separate companies, one focused on its food brands (e.g. Sara Lee, Hillshire Farm, Jimmy Dean), with the other managing its beverage brands (e.g. Douwe Egberts, Senseo, Pickwick).

2. **You are unlikely to be able to achieve a market-leading position**. If your strategies and plans do not suggest that you can achieve the benefits associated with being one of the top two or three players in the business's chosen market, that is a second sign that it may be of more value sold than kept. Given your other priorities and objectives, how important is it that you maintain your investment in the business, or could your capital, your energies and your focus be better spent on your other business activities? Carrefour's inability to obtain a top three position in the South Korean grocery market, for instance, led its management to decide to exit the country in 2006, despite ten years of investment. The executives wanted to focus their resources on those markets where they were likely to find a winning market position and sustainable returns.

3. **The market is or is becoming structurally unattractive**. Whitbread's decision to exit brewing and pubs was based on its management's correct assessment that these markets were becoming less profitable. As a result the markets were consolidating and, for brewing in particular, the manufacturing, management and distribution of beer brands were becoming concentrated across a few global players, such as Whitbread's buyer Interbrew. Critically, however, an unattractive market isn't always worth avoiding. In fact it's generally easier to deliver profitable returns if you are advantaged in a poor market than if you're disadvantaged in a thriving market. That said, given the level of consolidation in brewing, Whitbread's managers realized that the business simply did not have the scale efficiencies necessary to generate meaningful profits.

4. **You are not able to give the business the attention it needs.** Even where the business is nominally on-strategy you may still decide to dispose of it if you have better opportunities for growth and your attention is likely to be focused elsewhere. In this situation, new owners and managers may be able to deliver more from the business, and selling it may be the best option. When I worked for the UK retailer Boots, for example, the company owned several other retail chains, including an auto parts and accessories business called Halfords. Unfortunately, Halfords was only a fraction of the size of Boots and its management team perennially struggled to get attention from the corporate bosses. It was only when Boots sold Halfords sold to CVC Partners, a private equity group, that it received the attention and investment that it deserved, and its rate of growth and profitability rapidly accelerated.

5. **There are highly attractive offers on the table from one or more bidders.** In simple economic terms you should sell your business if the after-tax sales proceeds are clearly greater than the your best estimate of the future cash flows from your ongoing management of it. Even profitable businesses may be worth more to other businesses than they are to you. There may be specific synergy gains or tax advantages that the buyer could exploit to realize more value from the business than you could deliver, or your potential buyers may simply be willing to pay over the odds for the business. We have already discussed several examples where the buyers simply became too optimistic about their ability to drive new value from their acquisition, and paid too much. But there are also examples of buying companies benefitting from synergies that just weren't available to the seller. Although we have seen that Quaker Oats paid several times too much for Snapple, the company had succeeded in creating value with its acquisition of Gatorade. By using Quaker Oats's marketing, sales, supply chain management and purchasing capabilities the company was able to grow the distribution, sales and profitability of Gatorade in a way that its previous owners couldn't match.

You will note that I haven't argued that just because a business is unprofitable this is a reason to dispose of it. If you follow the actions and steps I've set out in previous chapters you may find that a shift in its scope and competitive strategy, together with a more focused management of its growth agenda, is sufficient to return the business to profitability. You should seek to ensure that you are getting the maximum return you can from all of your investments. You must also, however, regularly review your portfolio of businesses to identify whether any of the five factors we've set out exist, and determine whether divestment of the business is likely to be the best long-term solution.

Key Points

- There is a broad spectrum of alternatives for working with other organizations to achieve mutually beneficial aims, each with their own benefits and risks
- Successful acquisitions are strategy-led, which means that you need to be crystal clear on how a potential acquisition will help you deliver your strategic objectives and deliver value to your business. Acquisitions are a time for hard headed objectivity, not emotional or ego-led commitments
- The level of integration of your newly acquired business with your existing organization will be driven by your rationale for the acquisition
- There are six guidelines for getting the most out of your acquisitions, which include ensuring that you have the senior leadership in place to drive the targeted benefits, having a clear roadmap to deliver the value quickly and ensuring that the leaders of the acquired company are positive about the deal and are communicating that message to their people
- Partnerships can offer a flexible route to growth, but require a shared belief in the value of partnerships, a clear win-win set of objectives, a good level of fit between the organizations and their leaders and effective ways of working
- In addition to new growth opportunities, you should also be regularly reviewing your portfolio of businesses to identify whether any might be of greater value to you as an asset to sell than to keep

Chapter 10

A STRATEGY IS NOT JUST FOR CHRISTMAS

Turning Strategy Into A Way Of Life

A Process for Effective Strategy Management

A key theme of this book has been to manage strategy on a continuous basis, and not to see it as some kind of one-off, annual event. Many of the examples and stories have highlighted how new growth ideas, decisions on investing in emerging opportunities, and discussions on the future direction of the business, are likely to happen outside of big, set-piece events. They take place in one-to-one meetings, ad hoc group sessions or even corridor conversations, and not just in formal strategy sessions.

That said, the quality of these conversations is increased immeasurably when they are complemented by a structured approach to developing and managing your company's strategy. When you have a clear view of your company's direction, its performance, its markets and its customers, the quality of your other conversations becomes so much greater. Decisions become easier and quicker, as you inherently understand which options are likely to drive your strategy and which are likely to hinder it.

Session	Frequency	Annual Time Investment
Strategy Summit	Annually	3 sessions @ 1-2 days per session
Growth Summit	Half-Yearly	2 sessions @ 1-2 days per session
90-Day Agenda Setting	Quarterly	4 sessions @ 1/2-1 day per session
Strategy Reviews	Monthly	12 sessions @ 1/2-1 day per session
Strategy Goals and KPI Reviews	Weekly	As part of operating review meetings
Strategy Communication	Daily	As part of everyday meetings and conversations

Figure 10.1: Strategy Development and Management Sessions

Figure 10.1 provides a template for managing strategy over the course of a year. You may wish to flex some of the timings. The key to success is to ensure that you are regularly reviewing your performance and that you undertake a more structured review of your direction at least as fast as your markets are changing. Let's take a look at some of the major strategy meetings from Figure 10.1.

Annual Strategy Summit

This is the in-depth review of your strategy, its establishment, its refinement and, if necessary, its replacement. At the end of these meetings you and your executive team should have a clear and aligned view of your organization's direction and your priorities for investment. You should also have a high-level plan that will turn your goals into reality.

You do not need a cast of thousands in these meetings, although I have led sessions with over 30 managers for a multi-divisional client. The people you need around the table are those who will have ultimate accountability for its delivery, which is generally the executive team. You can seek ideas and insights from others ahead of the session, and also bring them in to the meeting at certain points to provide input, but you should ensure that those who will be accountable for making them happen, make the big decisions.

As outlined in Figure 10.2 breaking down the strategy summit into three meetings, each lasting 1-2 days, provides focus for each part of the process and also allows your team to carry out the necessary analysis to confirm (or otherwise) your emerging ideas and hypotheses. Typically the elapsed time of this process lasts from 6-12 weeks, depending on your team's availability, the level of disagreement and change your are considering, and your ability to get the relevant pieces of analysis completed. I have completed the process in four weeks where there was a real sense of urgency to develop a clear direction. If you find that you are taking more than 12 weeks you may be starting to get lost in the analysis. This timescale may be appropriate if you are considering a major move away from your existing strategy, and you want to ensure you understand all the risks and benefits, but for most strategy-setting processes it is better to keep up the pace.

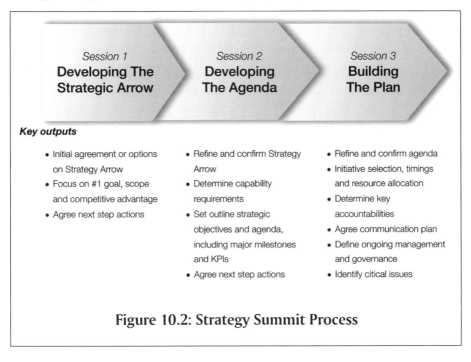

| Session 1 Developing The Strategic Arrow | Session 2 Developing The Agenda | Session 3 Building The Plan |

Key outputs

• Initial agreement or options on Strategy Arrow	• Refine and confirm Strategy Arrow	• Refine and confirm agenda
• Focus on #1 goal, scope and competitive advantage	• Determine capability requirements	• Initiative selection, timings and resource allocation
• Agree next step actions	• Set outline strategic objectives and agenda, including major milestones and KPIs	• Determine key accountabilities
	• Agree next step actions	• Agree communication plan
		• Define ongoing management and governance
		• Identify citical issues

Figure 10.2: Strategy Summit Process

The process set out in Figure 10.2 is as follows:

■ *Pre-Session 1 Homework.* Ahead of your first session meet individually with your top team, and other key players and advisers, to understand their insights and issues. Ensure that initial analysis is carried out and distributed to the Session 1 participants. The analysis should take the form of the reviews set out in Chapter 4.

■ *Session 1: The Strategy Arrow.* The purpose of this meeting is to create an initial view of your strategic direction, or, if necessary, some alternative views of the direction. This means that you should be looking to set out and gain initial agreement on your #1 goal, where you will play and how you will win. Ideally, you will also have a view as to your likely objectives and emerging strategic agenda.

The work in this session should use the analysis you've done to date to support or otherwise the team's opinions, but these are only there to support, not lead the discussion. Many strategy retreats I have attended start by going through a fact book, covering pages and pages of spreadsheets and PowerPoint charts on past performance, future projections and likely competitor activity. The only impact they have on the discussion is to dampen energy and enthusiasm. Effective retreats use your team's judgements and opinions as a starting point – call them hypotheses if you wish – which you can subsequently test.

It is likely, therefore, that you will have made several critical assumptions during this meeting. You should clarify these assumptions and agree what further work needs to be done to determine whether or not they are valid.

■ *Post-Session 1 Homework.* Take 2-3 weeks to assess the likely impact of the outline decisions made in the first session, undertaking relevant analysis and research, and seeking reflections and feedback from the team.

■ *Session 2: Developing The Agenda.* In this session you will confirm or refine the direction set out in the first meeting, based on the subsequent work you have undertaken. You should then determine the capabilities you will need going forward and use these insights to create greater detail and clarity around your agenda. This means that you will be proposing the initial set of initiatives and activities that will drive your growth, both in the short and medium term, making an initial allocation of accountabilities to take the work forward, and agreeing your major performance milestones and KPIs.

■ *Post-Session 2 Homework.* Again, take 2-3 weeks to confirm the hypotheses you established in the second session. You should also ask the team to create initial high-level implementation plans that meet your major milestones, performance improvements and resource requirements, to bring back to the next session.

■ *Session 3: Building The Plan.* In addition to confirming and refining the agenda you agreed in the previous meeting, there are four important elements to building the plan that you should focus on. First, you should confirm what is and is not in your initial program of initiatives, make resource allocation decisions across the portfolio of projects and confirm accountabilities and team structures. Second, you should define how you will communicate your new and refreshed strategy to your organisation and engage other key stakeholders. Third, you need to agree how, as an executive team, you will oversee and manage the performance of the projects and the overall agenda, clarifying meeting frequency, reporting requirements and executive roles. Fourth, you should create an initial list of critical issues that only the executive team can resolve to enable the teams to deliver their projects.

Once you have agreed the plan, you can then focus on its delivery through your reporting and project management processes, as we will discuss below.

Half-Yearly Growth Summit

Whereas the strategy summit is focused on clarification and creating focus, the growth summit is concerned with discussing options and opportunities, building alternative future visions for your organization. It should build on and feed into your strategy summit, and look at longer-term sources of growth and development. The growth summit is not, however, a brainstorming session: in my experience brainstorming sessions can begin the process of concept development but do not generally create the level of specificity you need for more general discussion.

The output of the growth summit is a short-list – probably no more than two or three – of new opportunities that the business will begin to develop, together with initial action steps. The objective of the session enables you to invite a broader-based group to the summit. In addition to your executive team, you should invite key players from your development and front-line teams, as well as external individuals who can offer new insights and ideas. The process of the session should run as follows:

■ *Pre-Summit Homework.* Assign managers to look at various trends and uncertainties in your market, who will report back to the wider team at the summit. In addition, collect any emerging ideas that have been discussed in your ongoing strategy meetings or other company forums that have the potential to make a major impact on the business over the next, say, five years. Again, ask specific managers to be ready to present these ideas and concepts to the wider group.

■ *Summit Agenda.* The meeting is all about getting a shared perspective on your markets and identifying ways you can win in the future. The opportunities are unlikely to be that urgent, which means that you can talk about them in more detail and seek to develop some real alternatives. You are also less constrained by your organization's existing capabilities and structures. Indeed, part of the agenda should focus on identifying the capabilities you are missing and need to consider developing or acquiring.

The 'meat' of the two days, however, should be focused on discussing the emerging ideas that your managers present. These presentations should be used as a starting point for further debate, building on the concepts and assessing them against the backdrop of your agreed market trends. You may have 10 or more ideas to discuss, and can use smaller groups to get into the details of the concepts. At the end of the two day summit the group should propose the shortlist of projects for the executive team to sign-off as the priorities for next-stage development.

■ *Post-Summit Activity.* The project leaders that you identify in the summit should then carry out initial development work on the short-listed ideas. This is likely to involve a mix of further desktop analysis and initial prototype development and testing. The aim of this work should be to assess whether there is likely to be a clear customer benefit and demand for the concept, and if it should be added to the formal strategic agenda. The teams should report back to one of the ongoing strategy review meetings or your quarterly review. You want to know three things: Is this a big idea?; Could the organization pull it off and, if so, with what risks?; and what's the likely level of investment and effort required?

90-Day Planning Sessions

New CEOs often talk about their first 90 or 100 days in office. In that period, they seek to get to know the business and allow the business to get to know them, build their team, develop key relationships, clarify the company's big strategic issues and get some early wins under their belt. But why stop setting yourself 90-day targets at the end of your first three months?

The purpose of the 90-day planning sessions is to refine your priorities over the course of the year, ensuring that your critical objectives are given the focus and attention they need in the light of changing circumstances. The meeting can be set up as an extended version of the monthly strategy sessions that we discuss below.

The output of the meeting is a set specific objectives and targets for the next quarter. It may be that you want to accelerate the delivery of certain projects and are willing to divert resources from other initiatives to make that happen. During the course of the year there will also be the inevitable unexpected events that have the potential to disrupt your operations. This session enables you and your team to refine and flex your organization's plans and priorities as you go along, and give you all the fresh impetus and desire to deliver the next wave of milestones and performance improvements.

Occasionally you may need to turn the wheel hard to avoid the oncoming storms and waves, but often all a boat needs is a light hand on the tiller to find the best winds, the smoothest water and the fastest route. The 90-day planning sessions gives you the opportunity to set your sails and set the direction for the next leg of your organization's journey.

Monthly Strategy Reviews

There are two objectives for your monthly strategy reviews. First, you should review the delivery of your agreed agenda, assessing the progress of your key initiatives and identifying and resolving critical issues. Second, you should review the company's major strategic issues in more detail. Let's look at each in turn.

In terms of your performance review, you should ask for a performance assessment for each of your strategic projects, using the report (or similar) set out in Figure 7.3. Use this as a basis for identifying critical issues and ensuring you spend sufficient time on those projects that are struggling so that your team agree on it as a plan to improve performance.

The review of strategic issues in these meetings enables you to keep on top of what's happening in your business and your markets without having to wait for the annual strategy review. For example, one of my clients identified their major issues as part of a strategy development process and then, over the course of the subsequent 12 months, undertook more detailed assessments of some of their major issues and opportunities which included their cost position relative to their competitors, how they could accelerate the growth of their on-line commercial activities, their talent development strategies and some initial research on export opportunities.

Critically, you don't want to tag these strategy sessions onto the end of your operational review meetings. In my experience, the immediate operational issues overwhelm the agenda and the time set aside to manage your strategic program quickly evaporates. Instead, set aside a separate day or half-day for these meetings so that you ensure that you give adequate focus to the long-term future of the organization.

These four strategy-related meetings – the annual strategy summit, half-yearly growth summits, quarterly 90-day planning meetings, and monthly strategy reviews – involve a greater time commitment to the management of strategy from the top team than I see in many organizations. That said, if you add up the total time required for you to lead these sessions, I estimate that it is in the range of 13-26 days over the course of a year, a little over 5-10% of your time. Given the impact that these sessions can have on your organization's long-term performance, and the importance that the CEOs that I've interviewed for this book place on leading the development of their company's strategy, I actually think that the time is relatively light. In fact, you may not get a better return on time in any other activity you undertake.

From The Top: David Johnston

David Johnston is the President and CEO of the EMEA region of Groupe Aeroplan, the $2 billion Canadian-based global leader in loyalty management. Among other business units David is responsible for managing Nectar, the UK's leading coalition loyalty programme.

We have made material progress in setting and executing our strategy by focusing on six key elements:

1. *Setting clear and ambitious goals that all the organisation understands and can focus on;*

2. *Defining what businesses we're in and defining success, both in quantitative and qualitative terms;*

3. *Providing our managers with a clear framework to help them improve and focus their strategic thinking;*

4. *Breaking down our goals into near term (Horizon 1), medium term (Horizon 2) and longer term (Horizon 3), so that we make sure that we make immediate steps to our strategic vision;*

5. *Clarifying the executive's team role and how it spends its time in three areas: people leadership, strategic leadership and execution leadership; and*

6. *Establishing and implementing effective meeting disciplines so that we are always focused on what we are trying to achieve.*

We operate in markets with a high degree of technological innovation. Our strategic approach enables us to balance our longer-term vision and plans with more immediate issues and opportunities. Critical to our success has been two factors:

1. *The fact that we've identified and agreed the businesses we're in – and also those we're not in. That way we avoid investing in technologies that are outside our core business expertise.*

2. *Ensuring that our strategic focus includes delivering the next 12 months' priorities. This makes sure that we stay relevant and avoids the 'big business' risk that the creation of a strategy becomes an end in itself, rather than as a means to delivering superior results.*

The Future Of Strategy

"In ten years' time will people laugh at us for developing three-year plans?" The CEO of a £300 million services business posed this question to me during a recent client meeting. *"Living quarter-by-quarter is madness,"* the CEO continued, *"But three-year plans are equally unrealistic."*

He had a great point. With the relentless rise in the turbulence and uncertainty in most markets it seems that the majority of long-term plans last less than the time it takes to create them! But, as we've repeatedly pointed out, plans and strategies are different. Our contention in this book has been that if you are unclear on what your business is trying to achieve and how it is seeking to win, you will simply be tossed about by the storms, swells and waves that will repeatedly cut across your markets and organization. Conversely, with a clear focus on your objectives, you can potentially use the winds to your advantage and can more easily steer clear of the worst hurricanes on your radar.

As we discussed in the previous section, however, you need to be flexible in the way you manage the implementation of your plans so that your immediate actions remain relevant both to your longer-term aims and your immediate priorities. That's why detailed three-year plans are no longer appropriate for most businesses, but a commitment and focus on delivering your three-year performance goals and critical milestones are essential. It is those companies that are rigid in their planning and unclear in their direction that suffer the most during market downturns, while those with both strategic clarity and the flexibility to respond to new opportunities and market conditions are the most likely to thrive.

Sustainable growth and success is reliant on three specific factors: a set of core commitments, a portfolio of future growth options and organizational speed in turning options into tangible results. Lets look at each in turn.

Core Commitments

You cannot avoid making commitments. These may be in the form of investments, organizational designs, customer propositions or operating models. McDonalds' has made core commitments to its portfolio of franchisees, its brand and its highly efficient supply chain. Similarly, Sony has made commitments to its research and development activities and specific products and technologies such as Bluray DVDs, while BMW has made commitments to the development and design of its range of automobiles and its investment in state-of-the-art manufacturing facilities.

No organization can avoid these commitments, but they come at a price: inertia. All businesses want to be able to turn on a dime, but once you have made a specific strategic commitment it makes it more difficult for you to respond to changes in your external environment. We have already discussed how companies such as Kodak and Olivetti struggled as their markets were revolutionized by technological changes and new customer demands. The investments and commitments these companies made to their more traditional technologies and capabilities made it far more difficult for them to meet the new challenges and realities of their markets.

Your business will succeed when the commitments you make are aligned with your organizational capabilities, your target customers' needs and other market conditions. This means that your core commitments should be focused on the capabilities and sources of competitive advantage that you judge to be relevant over the longer-term, not just the next year or so. The questions you should be seeking to answer include:

- Which of our target customers' needs are unlikely to change over the next 5-10 years?
- Which of our capabilities and competitive advantages are likely to remain relevant, and which are likely to become less important?
- Which elements of our current business model will therefore remain valid, and which are open to question?
- Which longer-term investments are we willing to support and which should we avoid?

By periodically questioning the basis and assumptions on which your organization is built you are more likely to ensure that your business is sustainable. Focusing on your core commitments and letting go of businesses, teams and activities, some of which are likely to be emotionally important to your people, is vital to ensuring that you have the potential for ongoing success. But this is only part of the story. You also need to identify new opportunities, and create options for fresh routes to growth.

Options

The value of a business is determined by two factors. First, the value is driven by the expected future cash flows from existing operations. Second, value is also generated by the expected cash flows of the business's likely options for future growth. For young, new start businesses, all the value is contained within the options, whereas for more mature organizations the value tends to be driven by existing operations. The danger for companies, particularly when the future is so unpredictable, is that their options for future growth are so limited they are worthless.

You must, as the leader of your business, develop options for new growth. As we have seen in other sections, these options may be your potential to reach new customer groups, to access new channels, to enter new geographical markets or to move into adjacent product and service categories. As with your assessment of your core commitments, identifying your most valuable options requires your judgement on two criteria: your assessment of likely future customer needs and your analysis of the capabilities that you must focus on and develop.

Even where you choose not to invest in pursuing a particular option, possibly as a result of a decision to focus on other priorities, the option still has a value that will be reflected in your company's value. In turbulent, chaotic markets the more options you have the more likely it is that your organization will continue to thrive.

The key questions you should be discussing with your team and seeking to answer include:

- What customer, market and technological changes can we discern and what are the implications for our organisation?
- What specific opportunities do these changes create for our business?
- What scope (markets, customers, channels and geographies) should we set for our business to reflect our existing strengths and these emerging opportunities?
- What assets and capabilities do we have that can exploit these opportunities, and what new assets and capabilities do we need to acquire?

It's fine to create options, but they become more valuable when they are turned into actual profit streams. Turning options into profitable businesses does not happen in slow, bureaucratic organizations. In today's fast-paced world it requires organizational flexibility and speed.

Speed

When asked how he was so victorious in battle, Nathan Bedford Forrest, a US Civil War general, reportedly replied, *"I get there firstest with the mostest!"* In business the prize doesn't usually go to the player who simply gets their first, it goes to the player who gets there first with a great business model. You need to be 'first' *and* 'most'. Ebay wasn't the first or only on-line marketplace to be launched at the turn of the century, but it was the first that developed a financial and business model that enabled it to drive profit growth, and not just revenue growth.

Getting there first with most is hard enough for new start-ups, unencumbered with the inertia of previous commitments, but it is harder for existing and more mature businesses: harder, but not impossible. As we have seen throughout this book, companies such as Tesco, 3M, GE, P&G, Apple and BMW have managed to achieve sustained success through their willingness to take prudent risks and become the first to succeed in exploiting new market opportunities. They have managed this speed through their ongoing review and management of their existing commitments, working in-house and with other partners to create new growth options, and establishing focused teams to turn selected options into high-value businesses.

To grow at the speed of change you need to possess the right mix of strength and flexibility to turn your organisation on a dime. Three-year plans will not get you there; you need to be far more agile than that. The capabilities you need for future growth and success are great decision-making, execution excellence, organisational simplicity and partnering skills.

The key questions you must respond to develop the level of pace required include:

- What new options and opportunities, in line with our agreed scope, will deliver the greatest returns to our business?
- For each of these opportunities, how well placed are we to be the first to offer customers a compelling offer *and* support that offer with a winning business model?
- Can we get there alone or do we need to acquire or work with other organizations to ensure success?
- What steps do we need to take now to maximise our speed and effectiveness in exploiting these priority opportunities?

Conclusion: The Strategic CEO Revisited

We started this book with an outline of the role of the CEO in leading, shaping and executing strategies that deliver sustainable, profitable growth. We'll conclude the book by revisiting the behaviors you need to demonstrate to make that happen. You are in a unique position to guide the future success of your business, and its customers, employees and stakeholders. Your role in setting strategy and ensuring its successful delivery is a critical aspect of the CEO's job – along with embedding the organization's culture and values, developing top talent, and aligning your team's individual ambitions with the company's goals to unlock their full potential.

No one in the organization has as much leverage as the CEO. From the moment you walk into the building on your first day (and probably before), everyone is scrutinizing your actions and behaviors, looking for patterns and inconsistencies. Others will rapidly follow the standards you set, and I have seen the culture and attitude across several businesses change within a space of a few weeks following the arrival of a new CEO. The way you lead and manage your company's strategy is not only important to the strategy itself, but also affects how the rest of your people across the organization approach the setting of their teams' goals and objectives, and their determination in delivering them. As the philosopher, Albert Schweitzer, once said, *"Example isn't the main thing in influencing others. It's the only thing."*

In my experience, the business leaders who are best able to tackle and drive strategy, which I call Strategic CEOs, are those who display the following behaviors and characteristics:

- **Strategic CEOs continuously raise the bar.** Today's successes are not enough for Strategic CEOs, who are forever looking for ways to reach the next level. They know that this means that they must be continuously renewing their organization, ensuring that it is not only fit for today's battles but also capable of fighting tomorrow's. *If it ain't broke don't fix it* may be the rallying call of many managers, but Strategic CEOs know that *if it ain't broke it will be soon*. They focus less on resolving every minor problem with the current business, and more on developing a new, better business.

- **Strategic CEOs share a bigger picture.** Organizational action is not simply about detailed plans and budgets; it's about giving your people a clear direction and encouraging them to move towards it. Strategic CEOs are able to create and communicate that direction, distilling the complexity of their company's operations and markets into a few overarching objectives and reasons to believe. They use metaphors and analogies and appeal to their organization's sense of what being at its very best really means, helping their people to buy into how the company can succeed and what role they can play to make that happen.

- **Strategic CEOs create options.** By raising the bar and sharing the big picture the Strategic CEO helps teams from across the business to develop new possibilities, to create new growth opportunities and to identify new options. They underpin the context they set with specific challenges to their people, encouraging them to go further and be more radical in their ideas. As new options are developed, they then select the best to drive the company's growth, accelerating it towards its strategic goals.

■ **Strategic CEOs relish the uncertainty and ambiguity.** They know that nothing is certain or forever in today's markets, but equally understand that the chaos and the turbulence will create as many opportunities as threats. Strategic CEOs will hold that uncertainty and avoid turning it into organizational anxiety. They are pragmatic optimists who are willing to shine the torch into the darkness and lead their teams forward. They know they don't and can't know everything, and are willing to say so, and are at their best leading in those situations that are the most uncertain.

■ **Strategic CEOs are consummate storytellers.** They love to talk about their business, share and explain its future vision, and use stories and anecdotes as a way of engaging their people and their stakeholders. They will highlight the small, specific actions that their people take to explain how they want the organization to deliver its grand plans. They know that people respond to emotion far better than they react to logic. Nobody remembers the detail of a pie chart, but they will remember the details of a story where a colleague took a specific action that exemplified the company's ambitions.

■ **Strategic CEOs are willing to make clear choices and trade-offs.** They know that they can't necessarily have it all and must choose how they wish to compete. They are as clear about what the business doesn't and shouldn't do, as what it should focus on. They understand that there are never enough resources to do everything, and that the key to success is to set priorities and focus the organization's efforts in the areas where it can have the greatest possible impact. Even though they keep the bar raised high, they seek to ensure that the organisation doesn't bite off more than it can chew.

■ **Strategic CEOs don't simply rely on the numbers for their insights.** They spend significant time with customers, colleagues and suppliers to drive their understanding of the business. They need to get involved in the detail, not simply to resolve immediate issues, but to take away important lessons that can help their company move forward. The reports and numbers they read tend to confirm the ideas they have already had from their front-line immersion.

- **Strategic CEOs embrace serendipity.** They deal with facts, rather than hope, but are also open to new ideas, possibilities and concepts. They use their strategy to drive their actions, but, at the right time, will also use new opportunities to shape their strategy. Strategic CEOs are continuously looking for how they can best exploit emerging successes and are willing to make the most of any fortunate discoveries to drive further growth for the company. Apple's exploitation of iTunes, 3M's success with Post-It Notes and Boots the Chemists' success with its Protect & Perfect skin cream range all involved a healthy dose of serendipity that their CEOs used to drive further growth for these businesses.

- **Strategic CEOs build a strong team around them.** They welcome the challenge that strong, well-rounded executives and managers will bring to their team, and don't need to 'do it all' themselves. Far from being threatened by executives with capabilities greater than their own skills, they build on and exploit others' strengths to drive the performance of the wider group. They know that if they set a clear direction and align the company's goals with their top team's personal objectives, they can focus their efforts on supporting their team's success, rather than having to drag the organization forward single-handedly.

- **Strategic CEOs break through the silos.** They will not allow functional barriers to get in the way of their company's success. They recognize that a great CEO is a great politician, and know when to compromise and when to stand their ground and take the tough decisions. Critically, they are able to help their people find common ground and work out a way where everyone can move forward together. Strategic CEOs build powerful networks inside and outside their organizations that allow them to draw on others' goodwill in difficult times.

- **Strategic CEOs hold their people to account and always follow-through.** Excellence in execution is critical to them, and they never forget what others have promised to deliver. They ensure there are processes in place that allow them to regularly review progress, identify issues and keep their managers focused on delivering what they have promised. Strategic CEOs don't allow their colleagues to wriggle out of their accountabilities, but demand that they focus on achieving the results. Where there are real issues, they focus on cause, not blame, and will support their teams in resolving the situation, but they will not allow weak and mediocre managers to drag down the performance of their stronger colleagues.

■ **Strategic CEOs are relentless**. They remain focused on finishing what they started. They are willing to take prudent risks and make mistakes, but don't allow setbacks in execution to dilute their resolve in achieving the objectives they have agreed. Their energy, passion and optimism acts as a beacon to the wider organization, motivating others to deliver more than they had previously realized was possible. As the company's goals are achieved, Strategic CEOs take time out to celebrate their success, but they then set new performance targets and objectives. They know that business growth is a Sisyphean task that never ends and are always looking ahead to the next challenge.

Being the CEO of any organization is not for the faint of heart. It requires courage, self-belief and an ability to inspire colleagues across your business to succeed. Developing and delivering your company's strategy is an integral aspect of the CEO's role and requires all three of these characteristics in spades. It is also, as we have seen, one of the most rewarding and powerful activities that you will ever undertake. You have the opportunity to create a new future for your business, your customers and your people, maximizing the impact that you and your company have on the world.

I am convinced that all organizations are able to achieve more than their people realize, but any success starts with the CEO and the top team setting a clear and distinctive direction. This book has provided you with the tools to provide the leadership and guidance to develop and deliver powerful strategies for your organization's growth. But only you can bring these tools to life. We need more great companies that have the ability to dramatically improve the lives of their customers and the wider world. In turn, these companies need CEOs with the capabilities and desire to go beyond business as usual; they need CEOs who can envision new futures, develop new markets, inspire their teams and turn their company's high-level ambitions into daily victories. In short, the world needs more strategic CEOs.

Index